Women workers in multinational
enterprises in developing countries

Women workers in multinational enterprises in developing countries

A contribution to the United Nations Decade for Women prepared jointly by the United Nations Centre on Transnational Corporations and the International Labour Office

International Labour Office   Geneva

Copyright © International Labour Organisation 1985

Publications of the International Labour Office enjoy copyright under Protocol 2 of the Universal Copyright Convention. Nevertheless, short excerpts from them may be reproduced without authorisation, on condition that the source is indicated. For rights of reproduction or translation, application should be made to the Publications Branch (Rights and Permissions), International Labour Office, CH-1211 Geneva 22, Switzerland. The International Labour Office welcomes such applications.

ISBN 92-2-100532-1

First published 1985

The designations employed in ILO publications, which are in conformity with United Nations practice, and the presentation of material therein do not imply the expression of any opinion whatsoever on the part of the International Labour Office concerning the legal status of any country, area or territory or of its authorities, or concerning the delimitation of its frontiers.
The responsibility for opinions expressed in signed articles, studies and other contributions rests solely with their authors, and publication does not constitute an endorsement by the International Labour Office of the opinions expressed in them.
Reference to names of firms and commercial products and processes does not imply their endorsement by the International Labour Office, and any failure to mention a particular firm, commercial product or process in connection with the technologies described in this volume is not a sign of disapproval.

ILO publications can be obtained through major booksellers or ILO local offices in many countries, or direct from ILO Publications, International Labour Office, CH-1211 Geneva 22, Switzerland. A catalogue or list of new publications will be sent free of charge from the above address.

Printed in Switzerland

PREFACE

This report is a joint effort by the United Nations Centre on Transnational Corporations (UNCTC) and the Bureau of Multinational Enterprises of the International Labour Office (ILO). It was specifically requested by the United Nations Centre for Social Development and Humanitarian Affairs as a contribution to the World Conference to Review and Appraise the Achievements of the United Nations Decade for Women: Equality, Development and Peace (Nairobi, 15-26 July 1985).

Dr. Linda Lim of the Centre for South and South East Asian Studies, University of Michigan, and the Economic Research Centre, National University of Singapore, prepared this study. The monograph has drawn on a wealth of published and unpublished material including the earlier research of the project co-ordinator. The joint units of UNCTC with the Regional Economic Commissions and the field offices of the ILO contributed material, and some governments carried out special surveys of developing countries for the present report. These contributions are appreciated.

Research assistance by Miss S. De Vries, Mr. T. van de Sande and Mr. A. de Kemp, in-service trainees with the ILO, is gratefully acknowledged.

TABLE OF CONTENTS

		Page
	Preface	
CHAPTER I.	INTRODUCTION AND BACKGROUND	1
	Aims, scope and methodology	1
	Women in development	2
	Development, multinationals and women	3
CHAPTER II.	WOMEN'S EMPLOYMENT IN MULTINATIONAL ENTERPRISES: A SURVEY	7
	Size of employment	7
	Direct employment	7
	Indirect employment	8
	Employment displacement	10
	Employment distribution	10
	By sector	10
	By occupation	10
	By region	10
	Employment trends	11
	Employment in selected developing countries	13
	Summary	13
CHAPTER III.	WOMEN'S EMPLOYMENT IN MULTINATIONAL ENTERPRISES IN AGRICULTURE AND AGRIBUSINESS	19
	The pattern of employment	19
	Conditions of work	21
	Wages and fringe benefits	21
	Hours and other conditions	22
	Labour legislation and regulations	22

		Page
	Impact of employment	23
	Expenditure patterns	23
	Living conditions	23
	Family structure and relations ...	24
	Job satisfaction	25
	Summary	25
CHAPTER IV.	WOMEN'S EMPLOYMENT IN MULTINATIONAL ENTERPRISES IN THE MANUFACTURING INDUSTRY	27
	Introduction	27
	The pattern of employment	28
	Characteristics of workers	31
	Age and marital status	31
	Education and work experience ...	34
	Rural/urban origin	36
	Summary	38
	Conditions of work and quality of life	38
	Recruitment	38
	Wages and earnings	39
	Statutory and other benefits	44
	Government legislation	47
	Hours of work	49
	Working environment and organisation of work	52
	Skills, training and promotion ..	56
	Job satisfaction and assessment	59
	Industrial relations aspects	61
	Employment security and job tenure ...	65

		Page
CHAPTER V.	WOMEN'S EMPLOYMENT IN MULTINATIONAL ENTERPRISES IN THE SERVICE SECTOR	75
	Introduction	75
	Financial and commercial services	75
	Tourism and related personal services ..	78
CHAPTER VI.	SOCIOLOGICAL IMPACT OF MNEs ON WOMEN WORKERS IN MANUFACTURING	81
	Income, expenditure and living standards	81
	Family relations	83
	Community relations	86
	Social and cultural impact on women	88
CHAPTER VII.	SUMMARY AND CONCLUSIONS	93
	BIBLIOGRAPHY	99

CHAPTER I

INTRODUCTION AND BACKGROUND

Aims, scope and methodology

This study has three aims: (1) to describe the employment of women by multinational enterprises (MNEs) in developing countries, specifically, its extent, distribution, and characteristics; (2) to analyse and explain this employment, paying special attention to aspects which are specific to multinationals and to women; and (3) to evaluate this employment in terms of its effects on women's working life, on their role and position in society, and on national development.

The report focuses specifically and only on women's employment in multinational enterprises - i.e. enterprises which operate in more that one country, etc.[1] In most developing countries this means foreign companies, since home-based multinationals exist only in a handful of them.[2] The general employment effects of multinational enterprises in developing countries have been dealt with elsewhere (ILO, 1981) as has the employment of women in general in these countries.

For reasons of space and data constraints, the report will primarily consider the direct employment of women by multinational enterprises in developing countries, although indirect employment effects are recognised and referred to where relevant. The impact of multinationals on women in other areas besides employment (e.g. as consumers) is, however, not covered.

The study concentrates on empirical issues and on the contemporary era. Detailed discussion of theoretical, historical and policy issues generally lie outside its scope. The report also attempts to be international in its coverage, although much more information is available on some countries than on others; generally more information is available for those countries which have greater multinational enterprise involvement and foreign direct investment.

A variety of sources are used, and are noted throughout.[3] Because of the disparate and scattered nature of some of these data, especially the lack of reliable and up-to-date statistics, most of the information and analysis provided will be qualitative in nature. The approach to evaluation will be: (1) <u>comparative</u> - comparing women's employment in multinationals with their employment in non-multinationals, with non-employment, and with men's employment; (2) <u>multivariate</u> - distinguishing the separate influence of the employer's multinationality on women's employment from other factors such as industry characteristics, host government policy, the local labour market, and indigenous cultural traditions; (3) <u>longitudinal</u> - considering trends over time with respect to employment conditions and women's positions. This triple perspective allows at least tentative conclusions to be made about the difference multinational employment makes to women's lives, how it is likely to change over time, and what it implies.

The study proceeds in the following manner. The next two sections provide a brief background discussion about women's role in development, and a short historical survey of the impact of multinationals on women's employment in developing countries. Chapter II outlines the current extent and sectoral, occupational and regional distribution of women's employment in multinational enterprises. Chapters III, IV, V and VI examine women's employment in multinational enterprises in the agricultural, manufacturing and service sectors, respectively. Chapter VII concludes with a summary of findings and a tentative evaluation.

Women in development

At least since the launching of the United Nations Decade for Women in 1975, the need has increasingly been recognised to consider women separately and to include them explicitly in the development process.[4] This would help to: (1) maximise the utilisation of domestic human resources for development; and (2) ensure that the benefits of development are equitably distributed between the sexes.

Women participate in, and are affected by, economic development differently from men. Their active role in and specific contribution to the developing economy is frequently underestimated, and they often benefit less from, are left out of, and even disadvantaged by, both market- and state-directed development.

Women have a dual role in any economy: (1) as workers engaged in direct production, in family farms and enterprises, commercial self-employment, and wage employment; (2) in the sphere of reproduction, as unpaid domestic labour servicing the family and household; this includes their role as consumers, the primary purchasers of market-produced items for household consumption.

In developing countries, distinctions between the spheres of production and reproduction are, however, often blurred, due to the high though declining proportion of non-market production and consumption which takes place within the family unit or household, and in which women are pre-eminently involved.

The argument is frequently made that government policy and market penetration in the process of development undermine women's traditional role in production, divorcing it from reproduction or reducing women's role to that of housewives alone. Where development does involve women in production, their position is usually subordinate and inferior to that of men in the labour force. Women workers are additionally overburdened by their continued nearly exclusive responsibility for unremunerated reproductive activities.[5]

At the same time, the argument can be made that development also provides opportunities for women to improve their economic lot and that of their families, and may help them to overcome certain oppressive aspects of traditional social relations. The potential at least exists for a diminishing of women's reproductive duties (e.g. through the reduction of family size), and for an increase in their participation in and rewards from direct production, especially production for the market. In this process women's unpaid labour may be replaced by, or transformed into, paid gainful employment.

Any development policy or process can thus be evaluated in terms of the extent to which it enhances or weakens women's economic position, improves or worsens their working and living conditions as individuals and as members of family units, and advances or retards the achievement of sexual equality in the legal, social and cultural as well as economic spheres of life. Such an assessment must be made in a comparative and historical context, taking into account also the great regional, national and local differences which exist among developing countries in relative resource endowment, economic structure and evolution, social organisation and indigenous cultural traditions. Such a context is taken into account in this report throughout the examination of the particular phenomenon of women's employment by multinational enterprises in developing countries.

Development, multinationals and women

The role of multinational enterprises in development has attracted much attention, research and policy debate for many years. Interest in their effect on women in developing countries has been more recent, although multinationals have directly and indirectly employed women since they first ventured into the Third World in colonial times and continue to employ them in many other sectors of the economy today (Michel et al., 1981).

Multinationals from Western countries in the colonial era were first involved in extractive activities in the Third World, such as mining, lumbering and trade in raw commodities, followed by plantation agriculture, all for export to world markets. The wage labour employed in these enterprises was mostly male, though in plantation agriculture especially, women were also found, as individuals or as members of family groups sometimes including children as well.

Besides such limited direct wage employment, the activities of multinationals also had many indirect effects on women's economic role. Where wage labour removed men from their homes, for example, women's role in operating family farms increased, and their labour often became the mainstay of subsistence agricultural production. Even where men remained at home, they were frequently introduced to cash crop production by multinational trading firms or their local - indigenous or expatriate - agents, and women remained mostly in lower-productivity subsistence food production.

The activities of multinational trading companies often had a disruptive effect on home-craft production and petty market exchange, which were traditionally dominated by women in many areas. Manufactured consumer goods imported from the industrialised countries took a greater share of the market than traditional handicrafts, and were distributed via formally organised commercial retail establishments largely run by male, often immigrant, entrepreneurs, rather than in the informal bazaar section run by women.

In the post-colonial period, most developing countries embarked on national industrialisation programmes based on import substitution, in which multinationals actively participated by establishing local factories. Both men and women were employed, the proportions varying by country and industry. Like the previous imports, the output of these factories, as with industrialisation in general, continued to compete with and often undermine traditional craft production dominated by women.

In the agricultural sector, commercial crop diversification and technological modernisation have had both direct and indirect effects on women's employment, again varying by country and crop. Jobs have been created for women in multinational fruit plantations and food-processing industries, for example. But traditional women's jobs in crop planting, harvesting and processing have also been destroyed by new mechanised technologies, in many cases developed and introduced by multinationals such as agricultural machinery manufacturers and other agribusiness corporations.

New extractive industries such as petroleum and lumbering, and their processing, in which multinationals were dominant, employed mostly men. The same is true of heavy industrial projects in which national enterprises rely on multinationals' technology and, often, capital as well. But more recently multinationals have increasingly contributed directly and indirectly to mass employment generation for women in labour-intensive export manufacturing industries in various developing countries. Their growing involvement in the service sectors of developing countries also creates jobs for women (ILO, 1981, pp. 21-25).

Thus multinationals have directly and indirectly both created and displaced employment for women in developing countries, the net effect varying by sector, country and historical period. During the colonial and early post-colonial period, they probably contributed to the net decline in female labour force participation observed in many developing countries as capitalist development proceeded (Boserup, 1970 and Chinchilla, 1977). However, such a decline would probably have occurred even without the involvement of multinationals under the general trend of industrialisation and modernisation, although perhaps at a slower pace and less extensively.[6] In the contemporary era, the net effect of multinationals on women's employment has changed and varies widely by country according to stage of development and the sectoral distribution of multinational activity, as discussed in the following section.

Notes

[1] "Multinational enterprises include enterprises, whether they are of public, mixed or private ownership, which own or control production, distribution, services or other facilities outside the country in which they are based." ILO: Tripartite Declaration of Principles concerning Multinational Enterprises and Social Policy, adopted by the Governing Body of the ILO in November 1977 (Geneva, 4th impr., 1982), paragraph 6.

[2] Examples are Brazil, the area of Hong Kong, India, the Republic of Korea and Singapore. See L.T. Wells: Technology and Third World multinationals, Multinational Enterprises Programme Working Paper No. 19 (Geneva, ILO, 1982).

[3] These include: an ILO special survey on multinationals in developing countries (1979), direct communications with various developing country governments, national and international statistical sources, reports and documents of international organisations (mainly the ILO), numerous country and industry case studies deriving from academic, union, church and media studies and reports, unpublished and ongoing research of the project co-ordinator and her colleagues (mainly in Asia), etc. These are listed in the footnotes and references.

[4] There is a voluminous literature on the general subject of women in development, which cannot be reviewed here. Boserup (1970) is generally taken as the starting point of interest within the international development community, and much varied scholarship has been conducted since then. For one fairly recent accessible collection, see Signs (1981).

[5] For a discussion of women's role in production and reproduction in developing economies, see, for example, articles in Signs (1981), especially Beneria and Sen (1981). For the project co-ordinator's analysis in a particular regional context, see Lim and Gosling (1983).

[6] A major reason is that women's reproductive responsibilities restrict their participation in wage-labour in the growing urban-industrial sector. Women are also vulnerable to technological displacement in the more slowly-growing agricultural sector where they are concentrated. See Lim and Gosling (1983).

CHAPTER II

WOMEN'S EMPLOYMENT IN MULTINATIONAL ENTERPRISES:
A SURVEY

Size of employment

Direct employment

Although precise statistics on the number of women directly employed by multinational enterprises in developing countries do not exist, a number of estimates can be attempted.

An ILO study estimated that 4 million persons were directly employed by multinational enterprises in all economic sectors of developing countries in Africa, Asia, and Latin America (ILO, 1981, p. 21). The regional distribution of this employment was as follows: 63 per cent in Latin America (2.52 million), 31 per cent in Asia (1.24 million) and 6 per cent in Africa (240,000). Between 1970 and 1980 the female industrial labour force in developing countries increased by 56 per cent. In 1980, 28 per cent of industrial workers in developing countries were women (Hopkins, 1983). Since approximately at the same time 87 per cent of multinational employment in developing countries was in manufacturing (ILO, 1981, p. 25), and assuming that the sex distribution of employment in multinationals was not much different from that in other enterprises, it can be estimated that women likewise accounted for some 28 per cent of the employment in multinationals in developing countries. Thus, the total number of women employed in multinationals in developing countries as a whole would be slightly over 1 million (1980).

Women are generally not employed in the extractive sector (for example, because of regulations in many countries prohibiting the employment of women in underground mines), but their share of total employment in agriculture and in services is greater than that in the manufacturing industry in most countries. In 1980, women accounted for 34 per cent of the agricultural labour force in Africa, 39 per cent in Asia, and only 9 per cent in Latin America. They made up 18 per cent of the industrial labour force in Africa, 29 per cent in Asia, and 16 per cent in Latin America. Women held 37 per cent of the service sector employment in Africa, 24 per cent in Asia and 39 per cent in Latin America (Hopkins, 1983). However, the bulk of women employed by multinationals would be in industry, followed at a distance by services, and then by agriculture. Most indirect employment would be generated by industry.

This pattern of employment contrasts with that of women's employment in developing countries in general, which is concentrated in agriculture. In 1980, 73 per cent of women workers in Africa and 70 per cent in Asia, but only 14 per cent in Latin America, were in the agricultural sector (see table 1). In Africa 9 per cent, in Latin America 17 per cent, and in Asia 18 per cent were in industry. The service sector employed 19 per cent of women workers in Africa, 13 per cent in Asia, and 69 per cent in Latin America (Hopkins, 1983). Thus multinationals may be considered to increase women's participation in the industrial sector, as they also increase that of men.

However, multinationals directly employ only about 0.5 per cent of the total labour force in the developing countries taken as a whole (ILO, 1981, p. 21). Only about 10 per cent of total world-wide multinational employment is in developing countries (ILO, 1981, p. 111). Since women account for roughly 30 per cent of this, it can be assumed that women in developing countries constitute some 3 per cent only of total world-wide multinational employment.

Indirect employment

Like all employment, that by multinationals in developing countries has indirect as well as direct effects (ILO, 1981, pp. 55-76). The former include multiplier and linkage effects, which may be expected to provide employment for a higher proportion of men than women, since men form the majority of the labour force in all sectors. In manufacturing, for example, materials and parts-supplying industries are likely to be less female-intensive than final assembly industries.

Indirect employment generation for women is likely to be greatest in the local subcontracting of labour-intensive production by multinational enterprises manufacturing for export from developing countries. This is most common in the garments industry, and in miscellaneous other industries employing mainly women, such as handicrafts and manufacture of toys, hats and artificial flowers. Women are employed either in small local workshops or in their own homes and paid piece-rate wages as part of a "putting out" network originating from multinational manufacturers, traders, wholesalers and retailers (Chapkis and Enloc, 1983 and Pineda-Ofrenco, 1982). However, it should be noted that not all subcontracting and home work for export from developing countries involves multinational enterprises. Much international subcontracting merely concerns international trade between national enterprises - local manufacturers in the developing country and importers or retailers in the developed country (Fröbel et al., 1980).

In general, indirect employment generation by multinationals will add to the employment of women, but this is limited by the tendency of many multinationals to prefer, for reasons of product standardisation, foreign sourcing of inputs. A probably generous overall estimate would be an additional 50 per cent which would yield a total of 1.5 million jobs for women directly and indirectly generated by multinational enterprises in developing countries in 1980.[1]

Table 1: Distribution of the labour force by economic sector and by sex in Latin America, Asia, Africa and the Middle East, in 1980 (in percentages: absolute figures for totals in millions)

	Men	Women	Men and women
Latin America			
Agriculture	40	14	34
Industry	27	17	25
Services	33	69	41
Total	100	100	100
(absolute)	88.4	26.4	114.8
Asia			
Agriculture	56.5	69.5	61
Industry	22	17.5	20
Services	21.5	13	19
Total	100	100	100
(absolute)	610.5	316.3	926.8
Africa and Middle East			
Agriculture	61.5	72.5	64.5
Industry	17	9	15
Services	21.5	18.5	20.5
Total	100	100	100
(absolute)	141	60	201
Total developing countries			
Agriculture	55.5	66.5	59
Industry	21.5	16	20
Services	23	17.5	21
Total	100	100	100
(absolute)	839.4	403.0	1242.4

Calculated from M. Hopkins: "Employment trends in developing countries, 1960-80 and beyond"; in International Labour Review (Geneva, ILO), July 1983, pp. 461-478.

Employment displacement

The activities of multinational enterprises in developing countries may also directly or indirectly displace some employment for women (ILO, 1981, pp. 69-70). This is most likely to happen in agriculture (especially through mechanisation), and in the import or import-substituting manufacture of modern substitutes for women's traditional craft production. Such displacement is difficult to estimate and is not unique to multinationals. It also results from agricultural modernisation and industrialisation by national (state and private) enterprises, though possibly to a lesser degree due to their usually lower capital-intensity. Multinational enterprise activity in the more recent manufacturing for export does not have a similar displacement effect since in most countries this is a new activity and there remains an excess supply of female as well as male labour.[2] Unfortunately it is not possible to assess numerically the extent of this employment displacement, whether attributable to multinationals or not, except to guess that it has probably decreased in net terms with the recent mass employment generation by the multinational-related export manufacturing industry.

Employment distribution

By sector

The bulk of direct multinational employment in developing countries occurs in the industrial sector (87 per cent), followed by "other sectors" (in particular commerce and services - 9 per cent), the extractive sector (3 per cent), and agriculture (1 per cent), according to an ILO survey (ILO, 1981, p. 25). This differs from the overall pattern of employment in these countries in being much more heavily concentrated in the manufacturing industry.

By occupation

The majority (60 per cent to 75 per cent) of workers employed by multinational enterprises in developing countries belong to the category of production and related workers, followed by clerical and administrative staff (12 per cent to 25 per cent), technical and professional staff (3 per cent to 11 per cent) and managerial staff (4 per cent to 6 per cent) (ILO, 1981, p. 33). This does not differ greatly from the structure of employment in non-multinational enterprises.

By region

Taking account of the data found in the two sections above and the differential rates of female labour force, as well as the general ILO estimates of multinational employment in the developing regions (ILO, 1981, p. 25), participation in each continent, roughly

50 per cent of all women employees of multinationals in developing countries can be estimated to be in Latin America, 45 per cent in Asia, and the remaining 5 per cent in Africa. Indeed the higher proportion of women than of total multinational employees located in Asia[3] than in Latin America reflects the relative prominence of such plants in Asia, and the greater importance of more male-intensive mining activities and import-substituting industrialisation in Latin America (Chinchilla, 1977).

Within these major regions, multinational enterprise employment varies widely and is largely concentrated in a relatively small number of developing countries and sectors of their economies. These are largely the extractive sectors of countries rich in natural resources (where mostly men are employed), and the industrial sectors of the relatively more advanced and newly-industrialising countries. These latter countries have large potential domestic markets, and are often important export manufacturing locations (in the latter, women are predominantly employed). The employment of women by multinationals is significant in Brazil, the area of Hong Kong, the Republic of Korea, Malaysia, Mexico, the Philippines and Singapore. Indeed, Malaysia and Singapore probably have more women employed by multinationals than the entire continent of Africa.

Employment trends

The ILO survey mentioned before shows that employment in multinational enterprises in developing countries has increased very rapidly since the 1960s (ILO, 1981, p. 21-22). Data retrieved from this survey suggest that employment opportunities for women have increased roughly parallel to those for men. Table 2 shows that for multinationals originating from four home countries and operating in the 40 most important developing countries in terms of foreign direct investment, the share of women in employment held steady or marginally increased between 1970 and 1977. The same pattern probably holds for multinationals of other origin (e.g. from the United Kingdom and the United States which account for more than 60 per cent of foreign direct investment in developing countries).

The future growth rate of female employment in multinationals in developing countries will depend on (1) the growth rate of multinational employment in general - which while it may still exceed the growth rate of overall employment in these countries is likely to be lower than in recent decades;[4] and (2) the share of women in multinational employment, which, as noted, appears to have remained fairly stable.[5] Differences in trends among developing countries would largely reflect sectoral shifts in the pattern of multinational employment, with the female share of employment increasing where female-intensive industries have increased in relative importance, e.g. in export manufacturing in Asia.[6]

Table 2: Employment of men and women in affiliates of foreign multinational enterprises of different origin operating in major developing countries of Asia, Africa and Latin America in 1970 and 1977

Origin of enterprises	CANADA				FED.REP.GERMANY				JAPAN				SWITZERLAND			
Year	E	Men		Women	E	Men		Women	E	Men		Women	E	Men		Women
1970	4	6 414	(91%)	640 (9%)	8	27 234	(93%)	1 926 (7%)	51	15 313	(67%)	7 472 (33%)	21	28 848	(82%)	6 491 (18%)
1977	6	17 787	(89%)	2 189 (11%)	13	51 073	(92%)	4 334 (8%)	108	57 697	(66%)	29 202 (34%)	21	51 575	(80%)	12 921 (20%)

E = number of enterprises included in sample.

Source: ILO Special Survey. The survey relates to a sample which includes more than 250 of the main multinational enterprises in 1977 (160 in 1970 and 90 in 1960) of 12 home countries (nine in Europe, viz. Belgium, Denmark, France, Federal Republic of Germany, Italy, the Netherlands, Sweden, Switzerland and the United Kingdom, plus Australia, Canada and Japan). It requested data for the years indicated on direct employment in the affiliates of these enterprises, in the 40 most important developing countries or territories (in terms of foreign direct investment).

For further information see ILO: Employment effects of multinational enterprises in developing countries (Geneva, 1981), p. viii, section A.

Note: For enterprises based in Canada, activities in the developing countries covered in the sample include mining, manufacturing and construction.
For enterprises based in the Federal Republic of Germany, activities in the developing countries covered in the sample include manufacturing, trade and banking.
For enterprises based in Japan, activities in the developing countries covered in the sample include agriculture, mining, manufacturing, construction, wholesale trade, finance and other industries.
For enterprises based in Switzerland, activities in the developing countries covered in the sample include manufacturing and finance.

Employment in selected developing countries

Tables 3 and 4 present data on the sex distribution of employment by foreign multinationals in selected developing countries for which longitudinal data was available from an ILO inquiry among labour ministries. They show that male employment considerably outnumbered female employment in all cases. A breakdown of the data (not shown here) shows that, for instance, in Chile, only six out of 46 multinational affiliates employed more women than men, and in India, only five out of 50 in the sample did so. None of the sample firms in Mexico employed more women than men. The firms in all these countries which employed more women than men belonged to various manufacturing industries, including chemicals, textiles, certain machinery industry product lines, film manufacturing, tobacco, tea, and rubber products.

Differences among countries, and changes over time, in the female share of multinational employment seem to be determined largely by the industry composition of the sample enterprises included. Thus the decline in the female share of employment in the standardised sample for India (table 3), from 36 per cent to 31 per cent between 1970 and 1977, reflects in the detailed analysis (not reproduced in the table) a 15 per cent decrease in employment in the tobacco industry enterprises in the sample, which had a higher than average proportion of women workers, and a 46 per cent increase in female employment in the male-dominated motor vehicle industry. Similarly, the increase in the female share of sample employment from 18 per cent to 23 per cent in Kenya reflects an above-average increase in employment in food-processing and related agricultural multinationals which had an above-average female employment share.

The non-standardised sample data for the six countries in table 4 show a declining female share of employment in all countries except Kenya. This suggests that female employment in multinationals grew less rapidly than male employment. However these data cannot be generalised, since they cover a limited time span and only a small group of heterogenous countries. They contrast somewhat with the much more global data presented in table 2 which suggest that the female share of employment as a whole in multinationals from the four home countries covered actually increased marginally. This may, of course, reflect the increased multinational employment, especially in industries employing mainly women in several important countries, such as the newly-industrialising countries of Asia, during this period.

Summary

In general, multinationals directly and indirectly employ a very small proportion - less than 1 per cent - of the female labour force in the developing countries taken as a whole. Women in developing countries account for less than 30 per cent of total multinational

Table 3: Employment of men and women by foreign multinationals in selected developing countries, in 1970 and 1977 (standardised data)*

COUNTRY	CHILE[1]		MEXICO[2]		INDIA[3]		KENYA[4]	
Year	Men	Women	Men	Women	Men	Women	Men	Women
1970	8 275 (78%)	2 338 (22%)	16 543 (77%)	4 917 (23%)	41 843 (64%)	23 642 (36%)	4 292 (82%)	950 (18%)
1977	8 370 (80%)	2 056 (20%)	18 738 (77%)	5 732 (23%)	48 074 (69%)	21 977 (31%)	7 770 (77%)	2 334 (23%)

* Same enterprises in 1970 and 1977.

Source: ILO inquiries among labour ministries.

[1] Affiliates of 49 multinational enterprises in mining, manufacturing, transport and services (especially insurance, banking and marketing).

[2] Affiliates of ten multinational enterprises in manufacturing, trade and services.

[3] Affiliates of 50 multinational enterprises in agriculture, mining, manufacturing, construction, trade, transport and services (especially banking).

[4] Affiliates of 20 multinational enterprises in agriculture, manufacturing, trade and services (insurance, banking and marketing).

Table 4: Employment of men and women by foreign multinationals in selected developing countries, in 1960, 1970 and 1977

	CHILE [1]			MEXICO [2]			PANAMA [3]			INDIA [4]			PAKISTAN [5]			KENYA [6]		
Year	E	Men	Women	E	Men	Women	E	Men	Women	E	Men	Women	E	Men	Women	E	Men	Women
1960	22	3 246 (71%)	1 313 (29%)	4	5 765 (67%)	2 902 (33%)	–	–	–	29	9 919 (80%)	2 416 (20%)	13	6 056 (97%)	173 (3%)	9	1 234 (78%)	342 (22%)
1970	52	8 275 (78%)	2 335 (22%)	10	16 543 (77%)	4 717 (23%)	23	1 056 (79%)	271 (21%)	52	32 741 (80%)	8 557 (20%)	23	11 326 (97%)	315 (3%)	22	6 674 (83%)	951 (17%)
1977	71	11 492 (84%)	2 258 (16%)	14	31 799 (83%)	6 545 (17%)	55	1 785 (82%)	404 (18%)	52	41 035 (84%)	7 638 (16%)	45	20 483 (98%)	479 (2%)	27	18 445 (81%)	4 389 (19%)

E = number of enterprises included in sample.

Source: ILO inquiries among labour ministries.

Notes:

[1] Affiliates of 71 MNEs in mining, manufacturing, transport and services (especially insurance, banking and marketing).
[2] Affiliates of 14 MNEs in manufacturing, trade and services.
[3] Affiliates of 55 MNEs in manufacturing, trade and services (mainly building).
[4] Affiliates of 52 MNEs in agriculture, mining, manufacturing, construction, trade, transport and services (especially banking).
[5] Affiliates of 27 MNEs in manufacturing and transport.
[6] Affiliates of 27 MNEs in agriculture, manufacturing, trade and services (insurance, banking and marketing).

employment in these countries, and thus for only about 3 per cent of total world-wide multinational employment. Female employment in multinationals in developing countries is concentrated in the industrial sector, but less so than male employment. The large majority of women employed by multinationals in developing countries are production and related workers, who account for a higher proportion of female than of male workers in these companies. Latin America has the largest number of women employees in multinationals - about half of the total found in developing countries (although it holds only some 40 per cent of the world's female labour force (Hopkins, 1983) - followed by Asia with a sizeable share (45 per cent) and by Africa (15 per cent).

Employment by multinationals in developing countries has been growing more rapidly in the past decades than employment by non-multinationals, for women as well as for men, and is likely to continue doing so, although perhaps at a slower rate than in the 1960s and 1970s. Employment growth for women in multinationals has probably kept pace on the whole with that for men, though this varies considerably by country, sector and industry. The sectoral and industrial distribution of multinational employment appears to be the main determinant of the share of women in multinational employment in any particular country. Multinational employment for women, like total multinational employment, is concentrated in only a few countries, and a few sectors of these countries, in the developing world. For these countries and sectors, the employment of women by multinationals is, of course, much more significant quantitatively and qualitatively than the modest global figures suggest. But globally speaking, the developing world multinational enterprises cannot be expected to be a major source of employment for the bulk of women workers.

Notes

[1] One study of multinational employment in the female-intensive electronics industry in Singapore estimated a total employment effect through vertical linkages of 1.4 to 1.6 of direct employment in 1980, depending on the company. See Lim and Pang (1982). Indirect employment generation is likely to be lower in developing economies which are less conducive to local backward linkages.

[2] Export manufacturing multinationals may, however, displace some female employment in full-employment situations where they attract labour away from national enterprises, which are then unable to survive. This has happened to some extent in labour-short Singapore.

[3] There is some evidence that multinational investments in Asia are more export-oriented than multinational investments in Latin America. See, for instance, UNCTC (1983).

[4] There are many reasons for this, e.g. the high growth rates of recent decades reflected the internationalisation of many companies from "newer" home countries such as Japan, which is unlikely to continue at the same rate.

[5] Women's share of multinational employment will also reflect trends in female labour force participation rates, which are expected to be fairly stable or to increase slightly in the developing world as a whole until the end of this century (ILO, 1980a).

[6] The available ILO data also show that the share of female employment in multinationals in a given industry appears to have remained fairly stable over time.

CHAPTER III

WOMEN'S EMPLOYMENT IN MULTINATIONAL ENTERPRISES
IN AGRICULTURE AND AGRIBUSINESS

The pattern of employment

The share of multinational enterprises in agriculture in developing countries is not very large as most of the investments of multinational enterprises are concentrated in the manufacturing sector. Moreover, the picture which emerges from the not very abundant data on multinational enterprises in agriculture in developing countries is that of relative stagnation. It can be concluded from this that their contribution to employment in this sector is also relatively small. On the other hand, the growing agro-industrial activities of multinationals may contribute in an indirect way to the development of agriculture-linked manufacturing employment (ILO, 1981, p. 8).

Women are employed in many differing capacities in multinational agricultural enterprises in developing countries. The most common employment is as unskilled or semi-skilled labour involving capacities which are learned on the job without formal training, for example rubber tapping in Malaysia, tealeaf picking in Kenya, and harvesting of fruit and vegetables like pineapples in Thailand and the Philippines, of bananas and vegetables in Central America, and of sugar-cane in many countries throughout the world.

Most of the women employees have little education and the structure of employment is such that there is little, if any, prospect of upward mobility for men or women. Women employees of multinational agricultural enterprises are also more likely than female employees of industrial enterprises, to be older, married or previously married, with children, and with less education. In most cases women work alongside men and often children, sometimes in family work groups, as is common in most traditional peasant production systems. Tasks are rarely exclusively female, though men tend to dominate in more physically strenuous work requiring muscle power, such as sugar-cane cutting, while women are more likely to perform tasks requiring manual dexterity such as tealeaf picking.

In some cases, such as rubber and palm oil estates in Malaysia, men are preferred for the more skilled and better-paid harvesting jobs, while women perform the lower-paid unskilled field jobs such as weeding and gleaning (Heyzer-Fan, 1981). The reason for this is that women - in this case employed almost exclusively as dependants of male workers - are regarded as secondary workers because their participation in wage-labour is constrained by child-care responsibilities. Institutionalised sex discrimination based on traditional patriarchal family structures and cultures is another factor.

Women are also employed in various agricultural processing and packing activities which frequently take place at or near the growing site, especially in large vertically-integrated agribusiness corporations. These tasks include elementary rubber processing, peeling and cutting of fruit and vegetables, their canning and packaging, etc., and are usually done mostly or exclusively by women. Such tasks resemble labour-intensive manufacturing tasks and may be considered part of the industrial rather than the agricultural sector - particularly as part of the larger food-processing industry - but they are performed by a rural-based labour force which, when engaged by a vertically-integrated enterprise, often alternates processing and packing with growing and harvesting activities, especially on a seasonal basis.

The preference for employing women in agricultural processing activities partly reflects women's traditional dominance in food processing due to their low wages and male labour shortage caused by male migration. Cultural and structural factors, important in other labour-intensive non-agricultural industry such as women's assumed greater manual dexterity and "docility" (see Chapter IV below), probably also play a part. One study of a foreign agribusiness corporation in Guatemala found that it explicitly preferred to hire women (at the same wage as men) not only because of tradition, but also because women workers were found by the employers to be more reliable and dependable, and more satisfied with their jobs (USAID, 1981).

Multinationals are not the most important direct employers of women in the agricultural sector of the developing world which in most countries still consists largely of small family farms. Large incorporated estates or plantations are generally owned by local state enterprises, following the nationalisation or state purchase of foreign-owned plantations in many countries[1] and the establishment of new state-owned large-scale agricultural plantations.

It appears that the sexual division of labour in multinational agricultural enterprises does not differ significantly from that in similar non-multinational enterprises. The number and distribution of female workers is determined much more by the particular crop or activity and by the country in which it is located than by the nationality of employer. Indeed, when states nationalise foreign agricultural enterprises, the sexual division of labour within them usually remains unchanged. Where multinationals employ women indirectly through various subcontracting arrangements with local farmers or processors,[2] the sexual division of labour in the subcontracted production generally maintains pre-existing traditional and/or contemporary local patterns.

Conditions of work

Wages and fringe benefits

The wages of workers in established estates or plantations are often set by union agreements or government legislation. However, this does not guarantee that wage differentials based on sex do not exist even where they have been eliminated in principle. In a British rubber estate in Malaysia (Heyzer-Fan, 1981), male and female rubber tappers have officially enjoyed equal pay since 1953; field-workers, however, only had their wages equalised by the union in 1979. As for the rubber tappers, equal wages are rather the exception than the rule. Sex differentials also exist as most of the women are employed as field-workers, who earn much less than tappers. Women with young children are usually employed as temporary or casual labour, paid on a piece-rate basis. On tea plantations in Sri Lanka women are hired for wages far below those paid to men for the same work.

Studies of women employed in multinational agribusiness enterprises in some other countries yield more favourable conclusions. A study of women workers in a provincial town in the Philippines found that line workers in a multinational fruit-canning factory earned nearly two-and-a-half times more than employees of locally-owned small commercial establishments, and nearly six times more than domestic servants (Costello, 1984).

The study of women directly employed in vegetable picking and packing by an agribusiness enterprise in Guatemala, mentioned before, found that both male and female workers were paid the same minimum wage of 50 cents an hour. As a matter of fact, women workers, who are considered more productive, seemed to have been preferred over men. Women employees' take-home pay ranged between 150 per cent and 300 per cent of that available in the two principal alternative paid occupations for women - domestic service and market sales, and more than wages earned by women working for domestic subcontractors to this same multinational. The pay matched the wages of the highest-paid male blue-collar workers (mostly construction labourers) in the area, and was much more than men could earn in farming, the traditional occupation of the rural areas (USAID, 1981). Wage differentials by sex probably persist in agricultural labour where physical strength may give men a productivity advantage over women working in the same job - most notably, in sugar-cane cutting in Mauritius (Hein, 1981) or in Jamaica (Standing, 1978) for example.

The higher wages and other benefits, where they are found in multinationals, are mainly explained by the fact that multinationals are typically large employers. And in most developing countries only large employers can and do pay the minimum wage and legally required fringe benefits.

Women employed in multinational agricultural enterprises in developing countries generally receive all statutory benefits, such as social security insurance, paid holiday and sick leave, and various bonuses (USAID, 1981). In some cases plantation workers are provided with fringe benefits superior to national norms sometimes as part of a tradition of low pay but high fringe benefits to maintain a cheap but captive residential labour force (Standing, 1978).

Hours and other conditions

Agricultural labour typically involves some fluctuation and seasonality of working hours depending on the nature of the crop. Thus rubber tapping in Malaysia must be done in the cool, dark, early hours of the morning, exposing women workers to the particular hazard of rape, since they work as individuals isolated from each other. Workers are also employed and paid on a daily basis, with the number of days worked and the associated income being low in rainy months and higher in dry months of the year (Heyzer-Fan, 1981).

The seasonality of agricultural employment means unpredictability of work and income in any situation. In Guatemala work in the multinational vegetable corporation referred to above is also seasonal, with women sometimes being required to work excessive overtime, long hours into the night, on night shifts, and on Sundays (USAID, 1981). One report from the Philippines cites a night shift stretching from 6 p.m. to 6 a.m. for women workers of a foreign-owned pineapple cannery (Perpinan, no date).

In a Malaysian rubber estate, with the introduction of equal pay women were no longer allowed to visit their children or return home to perform household chores while waiting for the latex to drip. They also had to perform potentially hazardous "ladder tapping" (carrying around, and tapping from, a four-foot ladder, sometimes on hilly ground). These conditions are no different from those prevailing for men, but affect women more adversely because of their added responsibility for the reproductive function and role. Other agricultural labour is also physically arduous - either requiring the exercise of muscle power (e.g. sugar-cane cutting) or constant bending and stooping in the hot sun (e.g. fruit and vegetable picking). Cannery work is also unpleasant and often dangerous, with fast-moving machines, and constant contact with fruit acids and processing chemicals causing skin rashes and respiratory ailments.

Labour legislation and regulations

Multinational agricultural enterprises are subject to the same government labour legislation and safety and health regulations as other companies, and are more likely than smaller local employers to observe them, particularly in the rural sector. In some cases, because plantations have been established for a long time - since the colonial period - their employment and labour practices may be subject to more legislative control and regulation than other enterprises, including those in industry.

Because of their long establishment and large size, agricultural export plantations, including those owned or formerly owned by multinationals, are often more likely to be unionised than other enterprises in a developing country.

The National Union of Plantation Workers in Malaysia, for example, is the largest employee trade union in the country, with 50 per cent of the rubber estate workforce belonging to it (Heyzer-Fan, 1981). Indeed, the high participation of women in union movements in Malaysia and Sri Lanka, where they account for half of the total union membership, reflects the high ratio of women plantation workers (employed mainly in multinational but also in state and local private enterprises). Women are also active, and take the role of leaders, in plantation workers' organisations in the Philippines (ILO, 1982a, pp. 43-44).

Impact of employment

Expenditure patterns

Wages earned by women employees of multinational agricultural enterprises are used to support their families at subsistence level. In the case of the Malaysian rubber estate, and also in the Philippines (Heyzer-Fan, 1981 and Perpinan), the male wage is inadequate to support a family, and the earnings of dependent wives and daughters are essential for family survival. Moreover, a high percentage of the households in developing countries are female-headed, especially in the Caribbean region but also in other parts of Latin America and Africa. In the case of the vegetable corporation in Guatemala, 40 per cent of the workers had children but no husband, making them the primary income-earner for their family unit, while another 21 per cent were married with husband and children. Single women contributed to their parental families, with whom they mostly resided. Income over that required for necessities and child-care was spent on fashionable clothing, home improvements, and entertainment (USAID, 1981). In the Philippines, as certainly elsewhere, single female migrant workers are reported to remit substantial parts of their income to their families (Perpinan, no date).

Living conditions

Plantation workers frequently live in employer-provided housing at the work site, as in rubber estates in Malaysia, where some new housing schemes with piped water and electricity are being provided. Such housing is often necessary given the isolated location of the work site, and its occupation is contingent on employment by the company. Other on-site services frequently provided by plantations are health clinics or hospitals, schools for workers' children, creches, and company stores, mostly at low standards.

In Guatemala, female employees of the multinational referred to above lived in private housing, mostly in parental (45 per cent), nuclear (17 per cent) or extended (12 per cent) households, in the surrounding rural area or nearby small towns. One-quarter lived alone, or with a female friend and/or their young children. In more remotely-located enterprises or those employing migrant workers, such as some banana and pineapple corporations in Asia, workers may be housed in company dormitories, often under crowded conditions.^{3}

In plantations, creche facilities may be provided by the employer, but they frequently seem so inadequate that workers may prefer to care for their young children at home. Often it is older daughters who are forced to drop out early from school to care for younger siblings, so that the mother may earn her much-needed wage for the family (Heyzer-Fan, 1981).

Family structure and relations

In plantations employing family labour, the employment of women is contingent upon their status as dependants of husbands or fathers, and the motivation for employment is to contribute to the family's subsistence. Family structure and relations do not change: the man is still dominant in the family in both status and income, and the woman continues to reside at home while working, and to have full responsibility for child-raising and housekeeping. This is the situation, for example, in the Malaysian rubber estate.

In the Guatemalan case, the situation is quite different and complex. On the one hand, employment of women in the agribusiness multinational has apparently reduced their economic power within the family by eliminating their traditional role as marketers of the family's - and men's - products. Men now subcontract agricultural production for the company, sell to it directly and are paid by it. Women now spend more time in agricultural work and less time on both marketing and household duties. On the other hand, the independent wage income has obviously freed women from economic dependency on their fathers or husbands, leading to a change in family relations and a reorganisation of family structures. The women now retain ultimate control over their income, and as important supporters of their households are accorded more importance, treated with more respect by other family members, and assume a central role in family decisions. Most notably, many women have started single-parent households of their own, or have begun nuclear households.^{4} In many other cases it may be held, however, that women's earnings are controlled by the male members of the family; thus, women's employment does not always imply real economic independence.

Job satisfaction

The Guatemalan study found that 95 per cent of interviewed women employees reported "high satisfaction" with their pay, their jobs in the multinational and their lives as working women in general. They valued the companionship of fellow employees and the "fairness and respect" of supervisors. The impersonality and standardisation of the multinational's management and labour practices was contrasted favourably with the personal relations characterising domestic service and working for small local businesses. Almost all the workers wished to continue working in their present job, although they disliked the seasonality of the work and the resulting unpredictability of earnings, night-work and excessive overtime. Freedom - from poverty and from traditional social relations - was the most appreciated consequence of their employment by the multinational. Workers who joined the company earlier and had been promoted were more satisfied with and committed to their jobs than later employees for whom promotion prospects were dim (USAID, 1981).

Summary

The case study information presented in this section is too limited to permit more than tentative generalisations about the nature and impact of women's employment by multinational enterprises in the agricultural sector of developing country economies. It does suggest a great diversity of situations. The characteristics and conditions of employment - including the sexual division of labour in production - depend very much on the particular crop or agricultural "industry", on the nature of the activity, and on the country concerned. Multinationals differ from non-multinationals mainly in their larger size, entailing a greater tendency to observe local labour regulations and ability to pay higher wages (presumably because of higher productivity and profitability). Inequalities between men and women in the distribution and terms of employment exist, largely reflecting women's primary responsibility for reproductive duties, and discrimination based on this. Where these inequalities are being reduced or eliminated, it is mostly the result of labour market conditions favouring women - such as a local labour shortage and women's perceived greater productivity in certain activities.

Notes

[1] For example, in Sri Lanka in 1972 (see Kurian, 1982), in Indonesia in the 1960s, and in Malaysia in the 1970s (through mergers and stock takeovers by state enterprises).

[2] For example, see Southeast Asian Chronicle, No. 86, October 1982.

³ See, for example, Perpinan (no date) which mentions 24 women sharing one small room, eight sets of three-tiered bunks.

⁴ The authors do not consider in detail whether this is the cause or effect of wage employment, assuming however the latter. Ibid.

CHAPTER IV

WOMEN'S EMPLOYMENT IN MULTINATIONAL ENTERPRISES IN THE MANUFACTURING INDUSTRY

Introduction

As noted before, the large majority of women employed by multinational enterprises in developing countries are found in the manufacturing industry. Before going into a detailed examination of this sector, it is worth while to point out how it relates to multinational employment of women in developing countries overall.

First, while most of the women employed by multinationals are in the manufacturing sector, they account for only a very small proportion of all women industrial workers in developing countries, i.e. most women factory workers are not employed by multinationals but rather by national enterprises. Second, most industrial employment by multinationals in developing countries consists of male workers; women account for only a minority of multinational factory workers, as they do of all industrial workers, although this varies somewhat by country. Third, most industrial employment, like most industrial investment by multinationals in the developing regions is concentrated in import-substituting industry; investment and employment in export-oriented manufacturing is significant only in a small group of countries, predominantly in Asia. Fourth, most employment in export-oriented manufacturing in developing countries occurs not in multinationals, but in national enterprises, with a few notable country exceptions (pre-eminently, Malaysia and Singapore). Fifth, most employment in export-oriented manufacturing in developing countries - including export-oriented manufacturing by multinationals - is located outside export processing zones in which multinationals usually dominate.[1] Sixth, not all workers in export-oriented industry or in export processing zones are women; a significant minority in many countries and zones are men - particularly in heavy export-oriented industry and in male-intensive shipbuilding, which is an important export industry in the Republic of Korea and Singapore, for example.

At the same time, export-oriented multinationals, whether in export processing zones or not, may in fact account for the majority of women employed by all multinationals in the industrial sector, since they use relatively more female labour than import-substituting multinationals.

Thus, out of the some 750,000 women employed by multinationals in manufacturing in developing countries (see Chapter II), probably more than half a million may be found in export-oriented multinationals whether located in export processing zones or not (for export processing zones alone some 300,000-380,000 women can be estimated).[2]

The pattern of employment

Not unlike the situation in agriculture, women in developing countries are employed by industrial multinationals mostly as production workers in unskilled and semi-skilled jobs and labour-intensive processes requiring manual dexterity and little physical strength. Most men employed in industry are also found in unskilled and semi-skilled labour-intensive tasks, but their jobs are more likely to require some physical strength and less likely to require manual dexterity. Skilled, technical, professional and managerial jobs are relatively few,[3] and largely dominated, if not monopolised, by men (Maex, 1983, p. 53). This reflects sexual inequalities in educational attainment found in most developing countries (men are more likely to receive the higher levels of technical and professional training which qualify them for higher-level jobs), and some degree of institutionalised sex discrimination in all (not only multinational, or industrial) employment.

The sexual division of labour in industrial employment in developing countries - as to a lesser extent also in developed countries - varies by sector and industry. "Heavy" industry, e.g. iron and steel, machinery and equipment, automobiles, shipbuilding, petroleum refining, other raw material processing, petrochemicals, etc., tends to be intensive in the use of male labour, while "light" industry, e.g. food processing, textiles, garments, footwear, tobacco, pharmaceuticals and other consumer goods manufacture, tends to employ a higher proportion - though not necessarily a majority - of women.

Women's share of industrial employment in any developing country thus depends to a large extent on the industrial composition of the manufacturing sector. But while "heavy" industry rarely employs any women, "light" industry in these countries frequently employs men to a substantial degree, reflecting both the lower participation of women in the labour force in general and in the industrial sector in particular (see Chapter II above), and an excess supply of male labour (these two are related phenomena). Cultural factors are often important; for example, in many Muslim countries the share of women in the industrial labour force and in wage employment generally is extremely low.

The sex distribution of employment in multinationals is also determined largely by local labour market conditions. In a given industry, local labour market conditions in most developing countries generally imply a higher ratio of men and a lower ratio of women than in industrialised countries. There is no evidence that, in the same industry and in the same developing country, the sex distribution of employment in multinational enterprises differs significantly from that of national enterprises.

Because of the industry and labour market characteristics referred to, multinationals appear to employ relatively more women in the few developing countries where they are concentrated in labour-intensive export manufacturing, such as the textile/garments and electronics industries. In effect, many countries host such manufacturing, but only in a few, small, resource-poor economies - such as Hong Kong and Singapore - does it account for the bulk of multinational employment. (Elsewhere the extractive and import-substituting industries predominate.) National enterprises in these industries, whether or not they are export-oriented, similarly employ relatively more women.

There are many reasons for enterprises - multinational or not - to employ mainly female labour in labour-intensive industries. First, the industries in question are traditionally dominated by women in both the home and the host countries of multinationals. Precisely because they are labour-intensive, they depend on low labour costs for their competitiveness. Female labour has historically been and still is cheaper than male labour everywhere. Furthermore, industries such as the garments industry and the food-processing industry replicate traditional female household tasks and utilise traditional "feminine" skills, while newer ones - like electronics - require a similar manual dexterity in which women tend to excel relative to men, largely for cultural reasons (Elson and Pearson, 1981). In many developing country peasant societies, manufacturing - mainly handicrafts - was traditionally the preserve of women and an extension of their reproductive tasks (Lim and Gosling, 1983). Modern manufacturing in a similar area of production, e.g. textiles, garments, footwear, represents merely an extension and also a replacement of this traditional feminine role.

Second, in addition to their assumed manual dexterity, manufacturers frequently consider women to be more productive than men in labour-intensive production because of their observed greater tolerance of, and better performance in, tasks which are repetitive and monotonous, yet which require a great deal of concentration, patience, precision and attention to detail (Lim, 1978b). Third, women are often also considered to be more reliable, less "troublesome" workers, more docile, less likely to organise and to generate or participate in labour unrest. In some countries they have actually been observed to have lower absenteeism and turnover rates, and they are generally considered to be more stable than male workers in, for example, Mauritius (Hein, 1981) and Jamaica (Standing, 1978 and Bolles, 1983). Fourth, because of their low expectations and lack of employment alternatives, and because they normally intend to work only for a short time, women are willing to accept and put up with "dead-end" jobs offering no promotional prospects.

Fifth, women's wages are usually lower than men's wages, and this lower labour cost enhances the competitiveness of labour-intensive industry. It is often considered acceptable to pay women less than men because they are not the primary breadwinners and thus do not have to receive a "family wage". In some countries, there are separate wage scales for men and women, and different minimum wages, with women's wages being lower. "Overcrowding" of the female labour market because of lesser demand - fewer job opportunities - for women also keeps market wages lower for women than for men. Sixth, because of women's relative lack of trade union organisation and political power, and prevailing cultural conceptions of women's wage-labour as being secondary both to their unpaid domestic labour and to men's wage-labour, they are often considered to be flexible, expendable or temporary workers who have higher voluntary quit rates and who may be more readily laid off in recessions than men (Lim, 1978b; UNIDO, 1980a; and Safa 1981).

Labour costs, efficiency, stability and flexibility are, of course, important in any industry, but more so in export-oriented industry which has to compete on the world market, whereas protected import-substituting industry can generally tolerate higher costs and more inefficiency. Export-oriented industry is also more vulnerable to falling demand and increased supply competition on a world rather than merely national scale, and the employment it generates may therefore be more cyclically variable, requiring more frequent layoffs which may be easier to impose on a female workforce. For all these reasons, both multinational and non-multinational enterprises which manufacture labour-intensive products for export from developing countries have a particularly strong preference for hiring women.

But women's cheaper labour and greater efficiency, stability and flexibility in factory work must itself be explained. On the one hand, the sexual division of labour and traditional patterns of feminine socialisation and acculturation in developing as in industrialised countries tend to emphasise attitudes, values, behaviour and activities among women which are conducive to their favourable work habits and characteristics as a labour force.

For example, domestic work builds in a tolerance for mundane and repetitive tasks. Food-processing and needlework develop manual dexterity and hand-eye co-ordination. Patriarchal family structures and relations instil filial responsibility, obedience to (especially male) authority, and an acceptance of female subordination. Idealised feminine virtues inculcate passivity, timidity and forbearance. Emphasis on marriage and motherhood as woman's primary destiny and duty limits female educational attainment, deflects women's commitment to wage-labour, reduces their expectations of job advancement, and minimises the unemployment problem as women who voluntarily quit or are involuntarily laid off readily leave the labour force and are re-absorbed into the home as "discouraged workers". It also keeps women's average wages low even where male and female wage rates are in principle the same, due to women's shorter job horizon and lesser seniority (since employment is likely to be temporarily or permanently interrupted by marriage, child-bearing and raising).

Differences in the sectoral composition of multinational employment and in local labour market conditions largely explain the differences among developing countries and regions in the importance of women's employment in multinational industrial enterprises. In absolute terms, most of the women employed by multinational industrial enterprises are found in export-oriented industries employing mainly women like textiles, garments, footwear, toys and electronics, and in only a handful of places like Brazil, Hong Kong, Republic of Korea, Malaysia, Mexico, the Philippines and Singapore (UNIDO, 1980a and Maex, 1983). A few countries with fewer multinationals employing a smaller number of women round out the total. They include El Salvador, Haiti, India, Indonesia, Mauritius, Morocco, Sri Lanka, Thailand and Tunisia. The dominance of Asian countries, many of them with home-based multinationals involved in these industries, is pronounced, but also other countries may have a high percentage of women working in multinationals. In El Salvador, for instance, women account for 39 per cent of total labour in multinationals, this figure being 52 per cent in textiles and 69 per cent in electronics (Report by the Government, 1984).

Characteristics of workers

It has frequently been pointed out that the large majority of women employed in multinationals in developing countries are young, single, fairly well-educated (by national standards), new entrants to the labour force, and include a high proportion of rural-urban migrants.[4] Each of these characteristics will be examined in turn.

Age and marital status

Virtually all the women workers at least in export-oriented multinationals are under the age of 30, and as many as 85 per cent under the age of 25. Between 70 per cent and 95 per cent are single, mostly never-married, women: the typical worker is a young, unmarried woman in her late teens or early twenties.

There is, however, considerable variation by industry, with the electronics industry having a younger workforce with an even higher proportion of unmarried women than the textile and garments industry. In Mexico, for example, the average age of women workers in the garments industry in the late 1970s was 26 years, compared with 20 years in electronics, and as many as one-third of the workers were heads of households (i.e. single women with children) (Fernandez-Kelly, 1980). Similar age differences between garments and electronic workers have been reported in some other countries such as the Philippines (Paglaban, 1978).

This largely reflects different educational and skill requirements in each industry. In electronics, especially in the semiconductor and other high-tech branches, a certain level of numeracy and literacy is required, and young women are more likely to have the necessary education than older women, given the relative recentness of mass education for women in most developing countries. In garments, on the other hand, industry-specific skills - such as cutting and sewing - are valued, and experience is more important here than formal education.

But in general most employers prefer younger women. There are several possible reasons for this. First, employers are often reluctant to pay the generous maternity benefits to which permanently employed pregnant women are entitled in most countries. Second, single women are both more flexible and more reliable workers than married women: they are free to work shift hours (particularly important in export-oriented industries and especially in electronics) and have lower rates of absenteeism due to family or child-care problems. They are also more mobile workers, able, for example, to migrate to remote locations such as some newly-established export processing zones. Third, young unmarried women are more efficient workers, since they have better health, eyesight and physical reflexes than on average older married women (important in both textile/garments and electronics), and are less likely to be fatigued from the burden of the "double day", i.e. having to combine factory work with unpaid domestic work at home.

Fourth, many employers believe that the married woman belongs in the home, and profess themselves reluctant to "disrupt family life". This is also true of multinationals anxious not to displease conservative traditional host communities. This has been found particularly for Japanese multinationals which in this connection have sometimes transferred sex-discriminatory hiring policies from their home country, as noted in studies for Malaysia. (Lim, 1978b and Smith, 1982). Fifth, employing young single women ensures a rate of "natural" or "voluntary" turnover when the women leave to marry or raise children. This tends to keep average labour cost low and is particularly favoured by labour-intensive industries with short learning curves for production workers.[5] At the same time, too high a turnover is disruptive, therefore very young workers may be preferred because they have a longer work-life prior to the age of marriage (i.e. a 16-year-old may be preferred to a 23-year-old).

All these are plausible and probably accurate reasons for the preference for young single workers also in other situations than those observed by the available studies. But they are by no means universal or uniform over different countries or even in the same country over time. Thus, for example, in a significant minority of developing countries, manufacturers in labour-intensive industries (whether multinational or non-multinational, export-oriented or producing for the domestic market) state a preference for married rather than unmarried women because they are considered more stable workers. Where married women work contrary to traditional norms, it is because they need the money to support their families, and in most cases are less mobile workers who cannot afford to quit their jobs. This is especially true of women who are heads of household (which is particularly common in the Caribbean) and the sole support of their children. In fact, women industrial workers include a much higher proportion of single women with children - whether divorced, widowed, never-married or separated from a male partner who has emigrated - than is found in the general population. In many countries also, where there is an excess supply of labour, older (and more experienced) workers may at times not be more costly than younger workers, but continue to earn only the minimum wage for many years (examples are found in the Philippines and Thailand).[6] There is a higher turnover of the female labour force which will keep it on average younger and with a lower marriage ratio than the male labour force in the same sector. Several studies[7] suggest that the higher female turnover is sometimes also encouraged by the employers or is a reaction to employment conditions.

There is a certain amount of illustrative information for some companies in a few countries. For example, a few Japanese companies in Malaysia appear to have incited single women to retire at the age of 25 (which is regarded in Japan as the traditional age for marriage) although faced with trade union resistance, this was not implemented.[8] In the Philippines a tendency has been reported for some companies (mostly non-multinationals) to keep women employed for long periods of time as "temporary", "probationary" or "casual" workers to avoid granting maternity leave and benefits and subsequently to lay them off when they have children.[9] But it cannot be concluded from anecdotal evidence alone that such discrimination against married women is a general phenomenon, or one peculiar to certain types of enterprises. Most countries in fact have legislation to prevent such forms of discrimination, although it is not always observed.

It has also been argued that poor working conditions and the intensity of work in multinational factories may cause workers rapidly to become mentally and physically "exhausted", so that they are forced to retire prematurely - for example, for fear of losing their eyesight in prolonged microscope work in the electronics industry.[10] Again this may be true for individual workers in some companies, but there is no evidence that it is a general phenomenon. In the same company and industry where some workers may quit early from "exhaustion", the majority seem to manage to work for long years without these problems (Lim, 1983b).

The most general and best documented observation that can be made here is that most women factory workers - in multinational and national enterprises, in export-oriented and import-substituting industries - quit work and leave the labour force when they marry or have children. The upper age limit of the bulk of the female workforce corresponds to the mean age of marriage or of first confinement. It is in fact the explicit intention of most young, single women entering factory employment to work only for a few years between school-leaving (or the minimum working age) and marriage. This is observed in most developing countries, ranging from Brazil and Mexico to the Republic of Korea, Malaysia, Mauritius, Morocco, Sri Lanka and Tunisia.

But again even this tendency corresponds neither to a universal nor timeless phenomenon; much depends on local cultural, economic and even individual circumstances. Where traditionally the economic role of women has been strong and female labour force participation high, where child-care support systems exist (for example, through an extended family network) and where the family's economic dependence on women's wage income is great, many women express both a need and a desire to continue factory work after marriage, and observed labour turnover rates in multinationals are low - for example, in the Philippines and Thailand. In Singapore, many working-class families rely on the woman's income to raise their living standards and this provides the incentive (as having fewer children provides the possibility) for women to continue working after marriage (Wong, 1982 and Salaff and Wong, 1983).

Cultural convention aside, it is mainly women's primary responsibility for the reproductive role - for housework and child-care - which causes them to withdraw from the workforce on marriage or childbirth. This responsibility makes it difficult if not impossible to perform factory work, indeed most wage-work in the modern sector, because it requires attendance in the workplace for long hours every day, away from the home and children. Women's traditional work in agriculture, the service and informal sectors, is generally more accommodating of the reproductive role since it is often spatially and temporally flexible. Thus, it is to these sectors that most married women turn when they are in search of wage income, leaving modern wage employment and factory work to younger, less encumbered single women.

Education and work experience

Many studies have reported on the relatively high educational level of women workers in multinational export factories in developing countries. In predominantly agrarian populations where few people have the opportunity to attend school for many years, virtually all these women workers have had at least a primary school education, and the majority in nearly all countries have had some or full secondary school education. In many countries such as Mexico, the Philippines and Thailand, many have even had some post-secondary education, including at times college or university as well as vocational training. The average level of education of industrial workers appears thus well above the general national average not only for female, but also for male workers.

Some earlier studies suggested that demand factors were responsible for this relatively high educational level of women workers in multinationals. Employers were said to prefer workers with more education even where it was not strictly necessary for the jobs they performed, because education was regarded a proxy for other desired workforce characteristics such as hard work, perseverance, ability to perform repetitive tasks, tolerance of authority and discipline, etc. Such personal/social characteristics are of course important in ensuring productive labour in the industrial setting (Lim, 1978b).

In fact, supply factors are now found to be more important in explaining the wide variation among countries in the educational qualifications of women industrial workers in multinationals. In situations of surplus labour in the local labour market, relatively well-educated women seek and accept low-skill factory employment because they have few alternative job opportunities. In situations of labour shortage, on the other hand, such women have superior job alternatives, and factory labour is left to the lesser-educated. Thus in countries like Mexico, the Philippines and Sri Lanka, where there is an excess supply of labour, the majority of women workers in multinational factories have completed secondary school, and a significant minority have had post-secondary education. In a labour-short country like Singapore, however, most workers in multinationals have only completed primary school. In enterprises in the electronics industry, for example, the co-ordinator of this study has seen the same manufacturing process being performed by part-time university undergraduates in Thailand, high-school graduates in the Philippines, mid-secondary graduates in Malaysia, and primary school graduates or even failures in Singapore. This variety of situations is also confirmed in other published research (Maex, 1983, p. 51).

In developing countries the spread of mass education in the post-colonial period has created for the first time a generation of young women with significant amounts of education, and with associated expectations of modern wage employment, for which they are now equipped. Traditional farm labour and domestic service are no longer acceptable to these women. Yet most are effectively excluded from the higher-level, white-collar, professional and semi-professional jobs to which they aspire - as clerical staff, teachers and nurses, for example - because of the excess supply of labour for these jobs (or, an insufficient number of such jobs), and various discriminatory practices. The very spread of formal education itself has also decreased its scarcity value.

Thus, in Malaysia, for example, women with a mid-secondary education would have qualified for many white-collar posts and nursing jobs two decades ago; but today the educational qualifications required for such posts have risen, and personal connections and influence are often required for admittance (reflecting excess supply and the preservation of traditional patron-client relationships). Modern factory jobs are a second-best alternative.[11] In Mexico, white-collar and service sector jobs are available to educated young women, but they frequently pay less than blue-collar factory work in multinationals (Fernandez-Kelly, 1983). In

Singapore, on the other hand, as alternative service sector jobs have been created - most notably in modern retail establishments such as department stores - they attract the better-educated working-class women, and over time multinational (and non-multinational) enterprises have increasingly had to accept women workers with lower educational qualifications, around the primary school leaving level.[12]

In a given labour market situation, however, most employers would prefer to hire the better-educated worker - up to a limit (university graduates and undergraduates, for example, are generally not favoured because they are likely to be both more mobile and more discontent). In a labour surplus situation, especially, educational qualification is a convenient "screening" device to reduce the number of applicants for each job.[13] The better-educated worker is also generally more easily trained, particularly in "high-tech" industries like electronics where technology changes rapidly and literacy and numeracy are required. In general, multinationals are likely to employ slightly more educated workers than non-multinationals, because of the better wages and working conditions they usually offer (see section on conditions of work below), and perhaps also a more modern "image".

Virtually all studies show that the majority of women working in multinationals in developing countries are new entrants to the workforce, i.e. they have no previous work experience which is not surprising given their average young age. However, a significant minority - between 25 per cent and 50 per cent (Maex, 1983, p. 51 ff.) have previously worked in other occupations which vary by country. In Malaysia and Sri Lanka, most of the previously employed have been factory workers; in the Philippines tailoring and service sector jobs are the most common previous occupations; and in Mexico service sector and even white-collar jobs, on the one hand, and domestic service, on the other, are common (Fernandez-Kelly, 1983). Hardly any workers joining industrial employment with previous work experience in any of these countries list farming as their earlier occupation.

Rural/urban origin

The rural or urban origin of women workers in multinational manufacturing enterprises varies by country and location within countries. Contrary to a common belief they are not everywhere predominantly recent rural-urban migrants attracted by the availability of multinational factory jobs. For example, in Cuidad Juarez in Mexico, 70 per cent of the maquiladora workforce are migrants, but only 8 per cent come from a rural environment; the majority have urban or semi-urban backgrounds, and most migrated as children with their families; only a small proportion left their hometowns as young women and with the explicit purpose of finding a job (not necessarily a multinational factory job) (Fernandez-Kelly, 1983). In Latin America factory workers are generally not recent migrants (Sala, 1983 and Bolles, 1983) and women working in multinationals are no exception.

A study of workers in the Bataan Export Processing Zone in the Philippines found that 62 per cent of all employees were recent migrants (Maex, 1983, p. 52). This is only to be expected given the rather remote location of the zone far from major concentrations of population. Most of the large export-oriented multinationals are not in fact located in Bataan but in the Metro Manila area, where they employ a high proportion of urban residents. Many of these residents may have migrated to the city earlier with their families, but before the establishment of the factories and without the explicit motivation of working in them. A similar situation appears to prevail in Bangkok, Thailand, and in Malaysia (Jamilah, various).

In Singapore, a small and declining proportion of women workers in multinational export factories are international migrants, mostly from neighbouring countries such as Malaysia, Sri Lanka and Thailand. They are found mainly in the textile/garments and electrical/electronics industries, where in 1980 they accounted for 27 per cent and less than 10 per cent of the workforce respectively.[14] Most of these foreign workers are from urban or semi-urban origins in their home countries. The Singapore workers themselves, like the Hong Kong workers, are virtually all non-migrants.

Thus the evidence is clear that the majority of women working in multinational export factories are not recent migrants, but established residents of the mostly urban areas where the factories are located. Most of the migrants are of urban or semi-urban origin, and rural migrants usually left the rural areas long before they took up employment in the factories. Only a small proportion of workers migrated alone as young adults in search of wage employment in general, rather than multinational factory employment in particular.

Host government policy often has a considerable impact on the employment of women migrants by multinational and non-multinational enterprises. In Malaysia, for example, the New Economic Policy requiring employers to employ workers in representative ethnic proportions has encouraged the employment of migrant Malays, since most factories are located in urban areas where Malays are under-represented relative to their national share of the population. (The majority of Malays are rural in origin and residence.) Rural-urban migration and industrial employment are seen as positive strategies to increase the participation of Malays in the modern sector of the economy (Jamilah, various years). In Singapore, the local labour shortage and a liberal policy towards migrant labour until 1982 encouraged the employment of foreign workers. Now, however, policy has changed towards discouraging the employment of foreign female workers in the labour-intensive manufacturing sector, as part of a national economic restructuring programme (Pang and Lim, 1982 and Lim and Pang, 1984).

Thus, to the extent that multinationals employ women migrant workers, they are largely responding to local labour supply conditions and host government policy. There do not appear to be compelling demand-side or employer-based reasons for favouring migrants over non-migrants, everything else being equal. Indeed the preference for hiring workers with a certain minimum level of education, and the common practice of recruiting via existing workers or other local "contacts" - especially in situations of excess labour supply - biases recruitment in favour of established urban residents with more opportunity for both education and contacts.

Summary

In sum, multinational industrial enterprises which employ women, like similar non-multinationals, whether in export-oriented or import-substituting industries, employ mainly young, single, relatively well-educated women of urban origin, who are new entrants to the workforce. There are considerable variations by country, industry and location. In more established enterprises and locations, in the textile/garments industry, and in situations of labour shortage, a higher proportion of older, married, less-educated and experienced women are employed. Workers' characteristics largely reflect the characteristics of the local labour market and, in some instances, of the host government employment policies. On the whole multinationals do not differ significantly from non-multinationals of the same vintage and in the same industry and location, with the possible exception of a slightly better educated (and therefore probably more urban) workforce. There are many similarities between the female and the male workforce in modern industrial enterprises, with the crucial difference that females tend to quit work voluntarily and leave the labour force at the age of marriage.

Conditions of work and quality of life

Recruitment

The most common way women in developing countries find employment in multinational manufacturing enterprises in through networks of kinship and friendship ties. Workers recommend their friends and relatives for job vacancies at their place of work, while urban-based kin in general help rural friends and relatives to find work by notifying them of vacancies. This happens everywhere - in the Republic of Korea, Malaysia, Mexico, Morocco and Sri Lanka, for example.[15] Employers, multinational or not, often encourage this pattern of recruitment, sometimes to the extent of paying their employees a fee or cash bonus for every new worker whom they introduce and who stays at least three months. (This seems particularly common in Malaysia.) This is a management device which not only minimises recruitment costs, but also creates a stable and cohesive workforce - in particular, it maintains the ideology of the family within the workplace, reduces conflicts among workers, eases the adjustment and assimilation of new workers, and diminishes costly turnover.[16] It is also a strategy used in situations of extreme labour shortage and hiring difficulty, as in Singapore.

A second common method of finding jobs, more frequently in labour-short situations and among newly-established enterprises, is direct recruitment by the enterprise which sends recruiters into potential areas of female labour supply. Sometimes contact is made with village headmen or government district officers to make a pitch to a community at large; sometimes a mass advertising campaign is conducted, e.g. by putting up posters; sometimes personal door-to-door recruitment is resorted to. Thus, in Malaysia, for example, new multinational electronics factories recruited vigorously in rural villages in the early 1970s. Once these job opportunities are known, and networks and linkages have been established between the factories and sources of supply, direct recruitment becomes less necessary. It remains necessary, however, where workers are recruited for factories in foreign countries which are short of labour, e.g. the recruitment of Malaysian and Thai workers for factories in Singapore, and of Colombian workers for factories in Venezuela.[17]

A third means of recruitment is via the mass media, mainly newspapers, which are more effective in reaching an urban rather than a rural labour supply. In urban areas companies also rely simply on posters and banners posted outside company premises.

In general, the tighter the labour market, and the newer the firm, the more vigorous and active are company recruitment strategies. Where there is a surplus of labour and factory jobs are relatively desirable, large numbers of workers go door-to-door in search of jobs, and many factories even have to post "No vacancy" signs. This does not always deter would-be applicants, and it is common to see crowds and long queues of young women lined up outside multinational factory gates in countries where unemployment is high and jobs of any kind are scarce. In such situations any jobs which become vacant are quickly filled by the recommendation of existing workers or other prominent local persons (e.g. the police in Sri Lanka),[18] or simply by "word-of-mouth" (e.g. in Thailand).

Wages and earnings

Wages and earnings for women workers in multinational industrial enterprises in developing countries typically range from a minimum of 5 per cent to about 25 per cent of wages for similar jobs and workers in their Western industrialised home countries, and a somewhat higher proportion of wages in Japan (Edgren, 1982, p. 17). This labour cost differential is obviously a powerful incentive for many multinationals to relocate labour-intensive production in developing countries to compete more effectively with local or world markets.   The ratio of profits to wages has been found high in some studies in developing countries (Ford, 1983, pp. vii-ix).

But multinationals do not appear to prefer systematically lower-wage to higher-wage countries in the developing regions. In Asia, for example, they are much more heavily concentrated in the newly-industrialising countries and areas like Hong Kong, the Republic of Korea and Singapore than in the lowest-wage countries like Bangladesh and Indonesia. Part of this may be cause-and-effect, i.e. the presence of large numbers of multinationals particularly in smaller countries exerts an upward pressure on market wages, which remain low where there are few multinationals to raise labour demand. But mostly it reflects the fact that wages are only one factor in the decision to locate.[19] Wage differentials also appear to have practically no influence on the choice of technology adopted by multinationals in developing countries (ILO, 1984d).

Wages paid by multinationals are largely determined by the local labour market conditions and, in some countries, legal minimum wages which vary by location within a country. In general, both market wages and legal minimum wages are lower in rural and labour-surplus areas than in urban and labour-short areas.[20] Wages also differ by industry - being generally higher, for example, in electronics (which both employs more educated workers and is a more productive and profitable industry) than in textiles and garments (Edgren, 1982, p. 17). And they seem to be (but are not always) higher in unionised than non-unionised enterprises.[21]

Wage payment systems can be complex, and workers' lack of understanding of their pay-slips is sometimes a problem which may lead to their dissatisfaction with their wages (Blake, 1980). Workers usually start out receiving a lower rate of pay - sometimes less than the minimum wage - until their period of "probation" (usually three to six months) is over. The basic wage rate for "confirmed" workers is considerably boosted by piece rates, shift premiums, overtime and incentive payments, bonuses (including bonuses for good attendance), cost-of-living allowances, merit and seniority increments, and mandatory fringe benefits such as health and social security payments. The basic wage itself may be computed and paid on a daily, hourly or monthly basis.[22]

Where workers complain about wage-payment systems, apart from their complexity, this generally falls into two categories. First, there are complaints about employers' non-payment of such items as legislated minimum wages, expected merit and seniority increments, overtime premiums, decreed cost-of-living allowances, government-recommended wage increases, and the like. Multinationals (with some exceptions found in smaller ones from other developing, mainly newly-industrialising countries) rarely omit such payments and usually follow the statutory or collectively agreed standards.

Second, workers dislike the flexible quota and target systems for incentive payments widely practised by multinational and non-multinational enterprises. Workers have to produce a certain output quota to receive their basic daily wage, or meet a given target to receive an incentive payment, but the quotas or targets may be progressively raised, making this increasingly difficult.[23] In other cases piece rates are occasionally reduced, or not increased in line with inflation and/or the market value of the product (Christian Conference for Asia, various years). Nevertheless, many workers prefer piece-rate systems, just as many prefer overtime and night-shift work, because it enables them to earn higher, sometimes much higher, than the usual wages.[24]

Wages also vary over time within a given country, industry or firm. Average wage levels and trends reflect workers' seniority, the length of establishment of the enterprise, and its fortunes in the market-place. Technological changes also have an effect - e.g. as labour intensity is reduced and labour productivity increased with automation and the shift to higher-value products, wages fall as a proportion of total costs and therefore tend to rise more. (This has happened, for example, in Hong Kong and Singapore.)

Probably the most important factor determining wage trends over time is the state of the local labour market. Thus, in a country like the Philippines where unemployment is high and increasing, workers even in some multinational factories do not receive seniority wage increases over time, but continue to earn minimum wages for many years. In some cases they are kept on as lower-paid "temporary" or "probationary" workers for extended periods of time. In Hong Kong and Singapore, on the other hand, and more recently in Malaysia, where full employment has been reached and has persisted for several years, labour shortages cause wages to rise more rapidly, especially for workers with seniority.[25] Unfortunately, relatively few women stay long enough to benefit from this as marriage and child-bearing withdraw many from the workforce.

Multinationals taken as a group almost invariably pay higher wages than non-multinationals in virtually all countries, including Brazil, Malaysia, Mexico, the Philippines and Singapore.[26] This is true even in the same industry, though much of the differential can be explained by different industrial composition (multinationals are more heavily concentrated in higher-wage electronics than in lower-wage textiles and garments), location (multinationals are located mainly in the largest urban metropolitan areas around capital cities, rather than in smaller provincial towns and remote rural areas), size (multinationals are larger and more profitable than most local firms), and worker organisation (multinationals as large enterprises are more likely to be unionised than the average local enterprise). Multinationals almost always pay at least, and frequently above, the legal minimum wage, which itself is sometimes above the market wage.[27] Where multinationals have been found to pay less than local firms, this was for instance because they were of recent implantation and their workers had less seniority than those in the longer established local firms (e.g. in the electronics industry in the Philippines in the mid-1970s (Paglaban, 1978)).

Joint ventures, from developing and newly-industrialising Asian countries, tend to pay wages similar to the local firms. These are generally smaller, economically weaker companies. This appears to have been the case, for example, with some of the joint ventures undertaken by Hong Kong, the Republic of Korea and Malaysia in the Bataan Export Processing Zone in the Philippines (Perpinan, no date).

A priori, one might expect wages in export processing zones to be lower than prevailing wages outside the zones, because of the concentration of newly-established firms and of export factories employing predominently a young and relatively cheap, female workforce. On the other hand, the massive increase in and concentration of labour demand in the zones - particularly where located in less-populated rural or small urban areas - might exert upward pressure on local market wages. In general, the two effects seem to balance out such that wages in export processing zones are in effect roughly comparable with wages for the same category of workers in similar industrial or other formal sector employment outside the zones. In some countries and industries - e.g. the electronics industry in Malaysia and the garments industry in Sri Lanka - they are even slightly higher (Maex, 1983, pp. 53-55). Wages in multinationals are usually better than in domestic enterprises located in the zones (Lim, 1983a).

Generally speaking, the wages in multinational industrial enterprises compare favourably with wages available to women in alternative low-skill occupations, such as farming, domestic service and the majority of service sector jobs. In large part this reflects the higher relative wage for modern industrial labour in general, as compared with agricultural and service sector employment, and self-employment in the informal sector (Christian Conference of Asia, 1984, pp. 31-32, Bolles, 1983).

But comparative rankings vary by country. In Mexico, for example, maquiladora workers in the border industrial zones earn more than many secretaries and salesgirls and there are some similar examples in the Philippines. However, in south-east Asian countries like the Philippines and Thailand, informal sector activities may yield higher incomes for those who succeed in them.[28]

Nevertheless, in most cases multinational factory jobs are relatively well-paid for the female labour force by general local standards. Even where this is not the case, they are frequently more desirable for other reasons such as better working conditions and higher status than, for example, farm labour and especially, domestic service. Sometimes factory work enables the women to make extra income. For instance, in some multinationals in Jamaica, women employees could buy products at a wholesale or special employee price, and resell them outside (Belles, 1983). In Curacao (Netherlands Antilles), women working at one multinational used contacts made at work with other women to expand their traditional informal sector activities, such as selling and trading in foodstuffs and handicrafts, and acting as agents within the factory for outside commercial entrepreneurs (Abraham-Van der Mark, 1983). Here, and in Indonesia (Wolf, 1984), the factory women set up rotating credit associations among themselves to receive occasional windfall income. In Malaysia, pyramid selling franchises for home products and cosmetics are increasingly becoming popular among women factory workers as they already are among women in other professions, e.g. clerical occupations. Perhaps more importantly, factory work is seen as stable employment providing a regular source of income. With that base of security, women can continue their informal sector activities and private enterprises outside work - such as doing laundry and seamstressing at home in Curacao, and running family hawker stalls in Singapore (Heyrer, 1982).

Women's wages in multinational factories can compare favourably with men's wages in similar or alternative male occupations. A <u>maquiladora</u> worker in Mexico, for example, can earn much more money than her father, as can electronics factory workers in Thailand (Bustamante, 1983 and Blake and Moonstan). Women working in electronics multinationals, in particular, can earn more than their husbands in typical domestic working-class male jobs, in Singapore and in Thailand (Salaff and Wong, 1983). Women in a multinational factory in Guatemala also as a rule earned more than most male blue-collar workers and farmers (USAID, 1981).

However, generally speaking, the average wages of women are still lower than those of comparable male workers, ranging from 50 to 75 per cent of equivalent male wages, even where equal wage rates prevail. In Malaysia, for example, wages of women in the manufacturing sector amount to only two-thirds of those of men in manufacturing.[29]

In most developing countries, the women's wages are therefore usually not sufficient to support a working-class family but are only supplementing family income. This is also true, however, of most male working-class wages or farming incomes - which is why most women have to work in the first place. The working-class family - typically a large, often extended, family with many children - survives with multiple income-earners. Multiple income-earning is in fact the norm in traditional peasant societies where the entire family - men, women and children - works the family farm together for subsistence. But in some countries today a significant minority of women factory workers are the sole supporters of their families, and survive at poverty levels.

While women workers in multinationals may not be paid a family wage, they are paid a wage usually more than sufficient for individual subsistence. Most workers not only fully support themselves, but also subsidise and contribute substantially to the upkeep of their families, whose standard of living and opportunities rise significantly as a result.

Finally, the real purchasing power of women factory workers' wages depends on broader national economic conditions, such as inflation and the exchange rate. In the Philippines, real wages have declined over time because of persistent high rates of inflation and unemployment, accompanied by several devaluations of the peso since 1972 (Paglaban, 1978 and Bello, O'Connor and Broad, 1982). In Singapore, on the other hand, inflation and unemployment have been low and the Singapore dollar has been appreciating over time, contributing to rising real wages.

In sum, female wages are usually lower than male wages in multinationals as in domestic enterprises, but this is the result of occupational segregation by sex, the lesser average seniority of female workers, and, in some cases, discriminatory wage scales set by host governments. Everything else being equal, wages in multinationals are on the whole slightly higher than, or at least not significantly different from comparable national enterprises. Wages in general tend to be higher where there are more multinationals, which have been longer established, and where the workforce is smaller; in such cases the demand for labour from the large number of multinationals, and their workers' seniority, are sufficient to push up wages. In the initial stages of establishment of female-intensive production - e.g. in export-oriented industries - when there are few multinationals and they are recent arrivals, wages are bound to be low, but they may be expected to increase over time as a result of the various factors analysed.

Statutory and other benefits

Many benefits - such as leave schemes, maternity benefits, insurance and pension fund contributions - are decreed by the host government legislation and vary greatly from country to country. Multinationals usually provide at least the minimum statutory benefits (and are better in this respect than some domestic enterprises). However as regards some of the benefits such as maternity leave (usually 30 to 90 days), sick and compassionate leave (paid in some countries, not paid in others), and annual vacation (ranging usually from a week to a month with pay) they rarely provide more than the statutory minimum.

Other benefits vary considerably, but usually include some of the following: health and medical expenses or in-plant medical care provided by company nurses and/or physicians, transportation or transportation allowance, food allowance or subsidised canteen, and free uniforms. The newer female-dominated (usually export-oriented) multinationals also frequently provide various social activities oriented specifically to feminine interests.

In a recent study in Malaysia of 50 large manufacturing companies employing mainly women (defined as having more than 200 workers, more than 50 per cent of whom are female), 29 of them foreign, in five female-dominated industries (electronic and electrical products, textiles and garments, rubber products, food products and chemical products), the following findings were made (Thong). Seventy per cent of the companies provided uniforms (84 per cent of the electronics firms); 66 per cent transport subsidy (89 per cent of the electronic firms); 40 per cent purchase of company products at a discounted staff price; 34 per cent gifts for occasions like birthdays, giving birth, and retirement (53 per cent in electronics); 26 per cent meal subsidy; 24 per cent annual dinners; 22 per cent free tea/coffee; 18 per cent interest-free loans to tide over periods of financial difficulties; 10 per cent organised excursions.

In the same sample, all companies provided medical facilities;[30] 98 per cent canteen facilities (the food supplied was at least 10 per cent to 20 per cent cheaper than that available outside); 84 per cent sports and recreational facilities; 38 per cent personal accident and health insurance coverage (58 per cent of the electronics firms); 30 per cent accommodation facilites; 22 per cent organised typing, sewing or language classes (37 per cent of the electronics firms); 20 per cent free film shows (32 per cent in electronics); 16 per cent library facilities (26 per cent of the electronics firms); and 8 per cent co-operative stores in company premises.

This array of benefits is generous by Malaysian standards, since only large, more prosperous firms are included in the sample. However, multinationals overwhelmingly fall into this category of firm and these benefits may be considered representative of multinationals employing predominantly female workers in this country, particularly in the most multinational-dominated industry - electronics. The situation in Malaysia is probably not representative of multinational factories with a high proportion of female workers in most other developing countries, although at least some of the types of benefits mentioned above are likely to be found in most multinational enterprises in Asia (Christian Conference of Asia (1981b)).

Two comments may be made in this connection. First, to some extent these benefits represent an attempt to attract and retain workers without raising wages as such. Second, only a minority of workers can actually take advantage of many of the benefits. For example, not all workers live in company housing even where it is provided (usually only for a small minority of the workers), nor do all avail themselves of company-provided transportation or recreational and training facilities where they are available.

Some of the discretionary benefits that employers provide are of importance for the functioning of the factories. For example, good medical care provided by the enterprise is useful not only for the worker but also to maintain an effective workforce and may in some cases attenuate fears of health hazards in the industry. In Malaysia transportation has often to be provided simply to obtain an adequate workforce because of the remoteness of many industrial sites, particularly export-processing zones, from concentrations of population, and because of poor local public transportation systems. Some workers may live as far as 45 miles away from the factory and have to commute for one and a half to two hours each way every day (Lim, 1978b). Transportation does not have to be provided in major metropolitan areas such as Bangkok, Hong Kong, Manila and Singapore. Some company housing has to be provided in Malaysia to encourage young, new, first-time workers, particularly from rural origins, whose conservative parents, for example, might be unwilling to allow them to live on their own in the big city. In Singapore company housing is provided mainly for foreign workers, mostly from Malaysia and Thailand. Singapore workers usually live in public housing provided by the Government and the factories are located in or near such housing centres. Uniforms are usually provided for reasons of safety and cleanliness, particularly important in an industry like electronics. The company social activities, as mentioned above, may attract female workers who are new entrants to the workforce, and may perhaps also reinforce feminine subordination to men which some studies find may reduce labour conflict (Lim, 1978b and Grossman, 1979).

A notable exception is child care, which in Asia at least is rarely provided by employers, even large multinationals which may employ as many as 4,000 women. Even in Singapore, where there is a shortage of female labour, where employers are trying to attract married women back to work, and where the Government is promoting workplace and child-care centres with capital incentives, apparently only one major private sector employer is known to have established significant workplace child care.

It has been argued that many of the benefits provided were sometimes of poor standard. This was noted in particular for crowded hostel accommodation, often with limits on the women's personal freedom. Hostel accommodation also tends to segregate women from the rest of the community, and to tie them to a particular employer, thereby restricting their mobility in the labour market. At the same time, it should be noted that hostel accommodation is frequently no worse than the workers' home living conditions, particularly for those from poorer and rural families. In some respects it may even be better, e.g. with respect to the availability of electricity and running water. Workers also save commuting time and travel expenses by living close to the factory; in some studies most of the workers are found to be satisfied with such accommodation (Zuhairah, 1983).

Government legislation

Next to labour market forces, government legislation and regulation are the most important determinant of wages and benefits provided by multinational and other industrial enterprises to women workers in developing countries.

Governments affect wage levels by setting minimum wages, decreeing cost-of-living allowances, and recommending wage increases. Not all countries have a minimum wage law. This is more common in poorer countries and the minimum wage is an attempt at least to provide a "floor" below which wages should not fall. In Asia, for example, Indonesia, the Republic of Korea, the Philippines and Thailand have minimum wage legislation, but more prosperous countries and areas like Hong Kong, Malaysia and Singapore, do not. Where it exists the minimum wage is often difficult to enforce and instances of non-compliance are frequently due to inadequate government supervision. Where the minimum wage is set at too high a level, added unemployment could be a likely result of full compliance with the minimum wage. In the Philippines and Thailand, for example, only a fraction of the urban wage workers appear to receive the minimum wage. Minimum wage rates are usually the same for male and female workers, with a few exceptions like Mauritius, Morocco and Sri Lanka where there are separate wage-scales for men and women.

Governments may affect wage trends by other means over time by varying the minimum wage or cost-of-living allowances but this does not necessarily mean an increase in real wages where an excess supply of labour persists. In this connection mention may also be made of Singapore, where the tripartite National Wages Council recommends annual national wage guide-lines whose effect in the 1970s was to hold down real wage increases, but which since 1979 have raised real wages in line with the government policy to discourage labour-intensive industries.

Besides influencing direct wages, some governments, e.g. Malaysia and Singapore, require employers to make social security, pension and/or insurance payments on behalf of workers. These are usually paid into a publicly administered fund. In Singapore, mandatory employer and employee contributions to the Central Provident Fund (CPF) - a government-sponsored compulsory savings scheme - total 50 per cent of the worker's gross wage, and substantially increase total labour costs. They may be used by the worker only to purchase housing, and may be withdrawn completely at the age of retirement (currently 55 years, but likely to be raised soon). The CPF contributions have enabled many workers to purchase their own public housing.[31]

Legislated paid and unpaid leave provisions differ from country to country, and relate to weekly rest days, public holidays, annual holiday (usually varying with seniority), sick and compassionate leave in most instances. They range in Asia from only unpaid sick leave allowed workers with a minimum level of seniority to 42 days' medical leave a year.[32] But some enterprises seem to have discouraged leave-taking by paying bonuses to workers who do not take their sick and vacation leave (Perpinan, no date).

Maternity leave is one legislated provision which applies only to women, and varies from country to country. In Sri Lanka, for example, a female worker who delivers a child is entitled to 42 days' leave (and 36 days' wages) for confinement. In Thailand, she is allowed 30 days' paid sick leave and an additional 60 days' unpaid leave. In Singapore, 60 days' paid leave is the norm. In the Philippines, paid maternity leave was shortened from 14 weeks to six weeks in 1974, and in Hong Kong eight weeks' paid maternity leave was legislated only in 1981 (unpaid leave was previously available). In India, maternity benefits can be extended to a maximum of 12 months. Some countries have introduced a limit to the number of confinements to which these provisions apply - usually a maximum of three or four. In all cases, women cannot be dismissed for or during maternity leave.

Various countries have other additional legal provisions related to women's biological functions. Many require that pregnant women be moved to light and non-hazardous tasks, and some require that nursing mothers be allowed time off during the day to breastfeed newborn infants - employers are then usually required to provide special nurseries for this purpose.[33] Indonesia and the Republic of Korea provide one paid holiday a month for menstruation leave, but this is often not taken because workers hesitate to submit themselves to company checks of this condition, or because it may cause them to forfeit good attendance bonuses (Mahnida, 1984). Restrictions on women performing certain kinds of heavy or hazardous, but generally well-paid, work are also common. For example, in Thailand women are excluded from jobs such as cleaning or operating heavy machinery, mining work, and carrying heavy loads, despite the fact that women in most developing countries have traditionally been used to heavy work, e.g. in farming and construction labour.

Finally, there are various occupational safety and health regulations which vary by industry as well as by country. Many of these are not yet fully developed in most Third World countries, and thus the standards in multinationals are often higher than the legislated norms, though still below those in the industrialised home countries. While government legislation and regulation may be inadequately supervised in many developing countries, it is usually observed by multinationals to a greater extent than is true for average national enterprises, and the minimum standards surpassed. This is not only because of multinationals' greater ability to absorb the costs involved, but also because of the world-wide experience of the enterprise (ILO, 1984c). Non-compliance by multinationals where it may exist is also more visible because they are typically larger and more prominent enterprises.

In general, modern enterprises particularly in the industrial sector are much more likely to observe the government legislation and regulation than small enterprises in sectors such as agriculture and services.

Hours of work

Hours of work are also legislated by most host governments, with a norm varying from 40 to 48 hours a week, and stipulated maximum hours and distribution of overtime in relation to the normal working week. Shift work is also regulated, e.g. minimum rest periods are required between shift changes, the duration of rotating shifts is regulated, permanent night-shift work is sometimes banned, and virtually all countries formally prohibit night work for women. The hours of prohibition vary but most commonly range from 10 p.m. to 6 a.m. or at minimum, 12 midnight to 5 a.m. It is shift-work regulations which most affect women working in multinational export factories where shift-work is common. However, export-oriented enterprises, multinational and non-multinational, can mostly obtain special permission from governments to employ women on night-shifts, sometimes subject to certain requirements such as that they provide transportation to and from work. The selective waiving of this prohibition has been very important in increasing employment opportunities for women. It is not peculiar to women factory workers, as employees such as nurses, night-time receptionists in hotels (Sri Lanka), telephone operators, bakery workers (Thailand) and rubber tappers (Malaysia) have long been exempt.

In most developing countries the normal working week in industry averages around 45-48 hours, but there may be variations. In the lesser developed countries with high unemployment and underemployment, the distribution of hours worked may be bimodal (i.e. many workers work only part-time because they cannot find full-time employment), while those who are fully employed often work long hours. There are also cyclical and seasonal variations. In Mexico, maquiladora workers averaged 48 hours a week (Fernandez-Kelly, 1984, p. 217). In Malaysia, one study of 50 large female-dominated factories found that 48 hours was the maximum worked in more than half the companies surveyed (Thong, p. 12). In Singapore, closer to 44 hours are worked and many multinational enterprises now work five days a week instead of the national norm of five and a half days. In El Salvador, the employees of multinationals work 44 hours, or five and a half days, a week (Government Report).

In some countries, extremely long working hours are reported for women factory workers (not necessarily always in multinationals) - for example, close to 60 hours a week in the export processing zone in the Republic of Korea, the Philippines and Thailand.[34] The hours in the Philippine Bataan zone are longer than those worked elsewhere, reflecting a concentration of mostly small local and other Asian Third World multinational joint ventures, and of garments manufacturers. Most multinationals from industrialised countries, particularly in the electronics industry, are not located in this or other export processing zones, and do not work such long hours.

Excessive <u>overtime</u> is the main reason for long working hours. In most countries overtime work is statutorily limited to two hours per eight-hour day, but waivers can often be obtained or the limits simply ignored. Hours are generally longest in the export-oriented garments industry, particularly in rush periods when deadlines on orders have to be met. For example, 70 hours per week and more have been reported during rush periods in Hong Kong, when garment workers on piece rate work till late at night or even overnight to meet orders. It may be added that long hours are common in smaller national enterprises.

Workers have to work overtime when required by the enterprise. It pays at a higher rate than normal working hours (usually one and a half times). For both reasons a high proportion of workers do work overtime when it is available. For example, one study of electronics factory workers in Malaysia found that 82 per cent do overtime (Zuharaiah, 1983). In Sri Lanka, the Philippines and Hong Kong workers are often practically compelled to work overtime in order to increase their wages (Maex, 1983, p. 57). The reduction or elimination of overtime in slack business periods can cause real hardship for workers. In Singapore, on the other hand. some years ago factory workers surveyed would only work longer hours at very high rates of overtime pay, as they had other higher-income alternatives (Heyzer, 1982, pp. 193-194). Today because of relatively high wages and job security Singapore factory workers still exhibit reluctance to work overtime even without alternative income-generating activities, and most overtime is worked by foreigners. Overtime and extremely long hours appear, however, much less common in the Caribbean and Africa than in Asia. The reasons for this have not been fully studied yet.

Apart from rush periods in the Hong Kong-owned garments multinationals mentioned before, there is no evidence that employees in multinational factories have to work longer hours than those in domestic enterprises; the reverse is probably true. All production workers do, however, generally work longer hours than white-collar workers. But women factory workers do not necessarily work longer hours than those in alternative female occupations. In the Philippines, for example, one regional study found that women working in multinational factories worked the shortest hours compared with two other groups of female workers: those in small-scale local enterprises in the commerce and services sector, and domestic servants, whose working hours are notoriously long (typically 16 to 18 hours a day, seven days a week (Costello, 1984)).

Besides length, the distribution of working hours is another issue. <u>Shift hours</u> are frequently worked in factories with a high female workforce, including in multinationals, particularly in export-oriented industries. The study of 50 such large enterprises in Malaysia found that 64 per cent of them worked on shifts, including 84 per cent of the electronics firms and 64 per cent of textile and garments firms (Thong, p. 15). In El Salvador, however, only 14 per cent of the multinationals worked in shifts (Government data). Rotating shift systems - with workers changing shifts every two weeks - are most common in many Asian countries and extra shift allowances are paid for the second (evening) and third (night) shifts. This pattern has also been common in Singapore, although with technological change and growing worker reluctance to do shift work, its incidence is declining. Many factories in this labour-short economy now explicitly advertise a five-day week and no shift work, in order to attract workers. Some American multinational electronics factories even advertise now a 38-hour work week (compared to the national norm of 44 hours), with higher overtime rates paid for all work over 38 hours. In both Malaysia and Singapore workers have been required to rotate shifts and permanent shift assignments are generally forbidden by government regulation, although as noted before it is possible to get this interdiction waived (Lim, 1978b). The situation is however not the same everywhere. A case has been reported that in a multi-national electronics company in Curacao workers were employed on three permanent shifts, all paid the same wages, and that workers were unable to change their shift assignment (Abraham-Van der Mark, 1983, p. 381). This situation seems to be, however, rather exceptional.

In most developing countries the three-shift system is not common, because of prohibitions against night work for women. Some workers possibly prefer shift work because of the opportunity to earn higher wages through payment of shift allowances, particularly on the late-night shift. Others, particularly married women, often appear to favour working on the second and third shifts because of the opportunity it provides to combine housework and child-care during the day with wage-work in the evening or at night (probably because child-care facilities are often lacking). But for most workers the shift system is physiologically and socially disruptive. For Malaysia it has been complained that the period of rest for changeover between the night and morning shifts was insufficient - 36 to 48 hours in the electronics industry, compared to 96 hours for hospital staff (Christian Conference of Asia, 1981b, p. 48).

Shift work is abandoned by employers usually where technological changes and/or labour market conditions make it unnecessary or difficult, as in Singapore and the acute shortage of female factory labour has prompted many employers, including multinationals, to establish part-time shifts for housewives to encourage them to return to work. The usual hours are from 5 p.m. or 6 p.m. to 10 p.m. or 11 p.m., enabling married women to perform all their household duties before reporting for work. Normal fringe benefits are provided for these part-time workers.

There appear to be no significant differences between multinationals and non-multinationals in the same industry in hours of work. Multinationals may be somewhat more concentrated in export-oriented industries, such as electronics, in which shift work and night work are common. But generally speaking they are less likely to work excessive overtime, and overall their hours of work are generally shorter than in most local factories and in other low-skilled female occupations as can be concluded from the various available studies. Differences in hours worked by men and women probably reflect differences in their industrial and occupational distribution, e.g. women may be more likely to work long hours or shift hours because they are concentrated in the export-oriented garments and electronics industry where rush periods more frequently occur. In Singapore, for example, three times more women than men do night shift work, and in the Republic of Korea, women work ten hours more per month than men.[35] But in Singapore also, the standard work week for electronics factory women has been declining and is now considerably shorter than the national norm for other workers, including higher-status workers like office and government employees, and professionals.

Working environment and organisation of work

The physical workplace environment varies considerably from industry to industry and enterprise to enterprise, but is nearly always better in the larger enterprises (whether multinational or not) than in the smaller enterprises. Multinationals from their experience in their industrialised home countries generally understand the importance of good working conditions for worker productivity, and as all larger enterprises can also better afford to provide these conditions (Blake, 1980).

Electronics multinationals, in particular, are well-known for providing good lighting conditions, air-conditioned plants, piped music, clean and adequate sanitation, fire protection, since as recently established enterprises they have a modern layout. Air-conditioning, cleanliness and fire protection are also necessary for the protection and proper functioning of expensive and sensitive equipment requiring a dry and dust-free environment; good lighting is essential for the efficient performance of visual tasks; and piped music (not always appreciated by the workers) may be used for facilitating or compensating for tedious, repetitive manual work. In the humid tropics, air-conditioning is particularly welcome for workers' comfort, though there are also complaints of being too cold in some factories.

Nevertheless, compared with most workplace alternatives for the young women, the physical conditions in multinationals are far better, for example, than labouring in the fields in the hot sun, in open market-places, and small local shops, and even in some of the workers' own homes, though not usually as good as in modern offices where white-collar workers work. Most large, modern local factories probably provide much the same amenities, especially if they are prosperous (Lorfing, 1983, p. 185).

Working conditions in the textile and garments industry are not as good as in the electronics industry, noise and dust being special problems for the industry. Small local enterprises, multinationals and joint ventures from other developing and newly-industrialising countries especially, frequently run textile and garments factories which use vintage machinery, are overcrowded, poorly lit and poorly ventilated, often with insufficient sanitary facilities and virtually no other amenities. Marginal enterprises often try to save on such overhead costs. Occasionally poor physical working conditions have also been reported in some large multinationals from the industrialised countries, e.g. because of facilities which were inadequately ventilated to cope with high temperatures generated by the combination of tropical weather and machine production (Robbins and Siegel, 1980 and Bradley, 1983). One of the enterprises in question finally installed air-conditioning when labour productivity suffered, and another moved to a new plant.

Some of the complaints of poor working conditions are related to the technology employed in particular industries. In the electronics industry, for example, the greatest concern has arisen over the use of microscopes which may cause eyesight deterioration, and over the use of chemicals in the production process, giving rise to skin rashes, burns and toxic inhalation resulting in nausea, dizziness, etc. There are also fears of being exposed to carcinogenic agents. Similar problems are also encountered in the industrialised home countries of the multinationals (Green, 1983, p. 307). On a different level, workers complain sometimes about the tedious, precise nature of production processes like manual assembly, requiring them to sit for long hours on the assembly bench, concentrating all the time on repetitive tasks.

While technology determines the nature of work and some of the problems, these may be compounded by the pace of work, which has more to do with management's desire for maximum efficiency. Not infrequently workers in electronics, textile, garments and other female-dominated industries complain about rigid regulation - including lunch breaks which are too brief (usually 30 minutes) and insufficient, non-existent or restricted rest-periods. Supervision is often intense and strick discipline is observed, both in multinational and national enterprises (Fröbel et al., 1980).

Three points need to be noted here. The first is that low wages are primarily responsible for workers' tolerance of poor working conditions and their compliance with a rapid pace of work where this exists. Workers often need to increase their wages by maximising their productivity - working long hours and very intensively in order to meet quotas and targets, not merely to keep their jobs in a situation of high unemployment, but also to earn incentive bonuses and high piece-rate wages. Internal motivation is thus at least as compelling as any external influence by management and supervisors. Sometimes workers eschew safety precautions where these may interfere with the speed of their production, e.g. the wearing of rubber gloves in fruit canning and chemical handling.

Second, women, who both expect to work for a relatively short period of time and have fewer job alternatives, may be more likely to put up with poor working conditions. Third, generally speaking, working conditions also reflect the state of the local labour market outside the factory. In a slack labour market workers are "grateful" for whatever job they can get. But when the labour market is tight, employers with poor working conditions are compelled to improve these in order to attract workers.

It has certainly partly to do with a tightening of labour markets as well as with technological change that in the multinational electronics industry in Singapore, for example, conditions over the past ten years have improved considerably. Microscope work is increasingly rare, as is shift-work and weekend work, and in some factories it may earn a premium. Workers use computerised equipment instead, and work-stations are increasingly individualised or grouped as the long rows of standard assembly lines become obsolete. There are fewer hazardous processes as workers refuse to do them, except at a much higher wage. Discipline in the new "high-tech" companies appears more slack, with workers allowed to walk around the floor, chatting with each other, and even playing their own individual transistor radios or cassette players. Uniforms are increasingly abandoned in favour of the workers' own more fashionable and individualised clothing, and the general impression is of a more diverse and relaxed atmosphere; machine-paced work and piece-rated work have largely disappeared (impressions from repeated factory visits by the project co-ordinator).

The role of legislation in the field of safety and health was discussed in the previous section. Methodology is a major problem in assessing <u>occupational safety and health</u> problems[36] among women factory workers in developing countries. First, there are few reliable statistics or large-scale surveys. Second, this is a multivariate problem, and one must distinguish the specific effects of work in a particular factory from other factors. Third, the incidence of various health problems among these workers must be compared with their incidence among other control groups. In the interests of this report, comparison must also be made between multinational and non-multinational enterprises, between male and female workers, and between workers in developed and developing countries. In the absence of such definitive studies, a few preliminary remarks may be made.

First, it is likely that women factory workers in developing countries suffer from more safety and health problems than similar workers in the developed countries. This is due to less rigorous safety and health regulations in the developing countries; to lower levels of education and understanding of the problems; to lower wages and greater economic need causing workers consciously or unconsciously to trade off danger, discomfort and inconvenience for additional income; to lesser worker organisation and the weak market power of unskilled labour; and to the generally lower level of health and greater exposure to environmental diseases in developing countries.

Second, some of the health problems of women factory workers are not work-related, but rather common to other working women in these countries. Such complaints as frequent colds, coughs, sore throats, headaches, menstrual pain and irregularity, fatigue, lethargy, anaemia, gastric problems, back pains, etc. are common to a large number of young women, particularly those who are under-nourished and overworked. It is often not clear if women factory workers suffer more from such common problems than others. In fact, they may be in somewhat better general health due to higher incomes, better working conditions and better working hours in comparison with some other groups of young working women. They also usually have better access to health care, particularly in the larger modern factories which provide company health care and medical services on company premises.

Third, even where women factory workers may be in worse general health than other women, this may not reflect workplace conditions, but rather the generally low socio-economic level of these workers. One study in the Republic of Korea, for example, reported that women workers' physique was inferior to that of women students of the same age (who are likely to be of a more fortunate socio-economic background). Women workers, particularly migrants from rural areas, lived in unsanitary environments and poor nutritional conditions (Kyu, 1979, p. 56). In other words, poverty rather than factory employment is the cause of many women workers' health problems.

Fourth, factory working conditions may aggravate, but not cause, basic health problems among women workers. Workers' fatigue, for example, does not result solely from factory employment, but often from its combination with other tasks that they also perform. For example, many workers must undertake a long and tiring daily journey to and from work. Some are forced to "moonlight" or take on second jobs - such as hawking food, taking in laundry or sewing - in order to raise their meagre incomes. Others, particularly married women and those with children, are responsible for housework and child care as well as wage-work. Still others spend their after-work hours studying to improve their education; in the Philippines and Thailand, for example, many women workers in multinational factories are part-time university undergraduates. It is often the combination of all these functions, in particular, women's "double day" and dual responsibility for both production and reproduction, which is the prime cause of fatigue where it is found among women factory workers. Fifth, several forms of employment available to low-skill workers in developing countries are hazardous in one way or another, for men as well as for women.

In general, one may conclude that working conditions in multinationals, which usually have a modern layout and an above-average safety and health record in developing countries, are more likely to be better than those in non-multinationals in the same sector and industry. However, better working conditions alone do not resolve women's quality of life problems where they are rooted in the dual responsibilities of women in production and reproduction.

Skills, training and promotion

The vast majority of women workers in multinational industrial enterprises in developing countries work in low-level, unskilled or semi-skilled production jobs. These jobs require no previous work experience and only little education (although more highly educated workers may be employed as shown in the previous section above). Training is provided on the job and learning curves are relatively short, with peak productivity for most jobs achieved within a year of employment. This varies somewhat from industry to industry, e.g. a higher level of skill, but lower level of education, is required in the garments than in the electronics industry.

Promotion opportunities for the average worker are rare, largely because of the pyramidal structure of jobs within industrial enterprises. In multinationals, the international division of labour concentrates most of the lower jobs in the hierarchy in developing countries, while retaining most of the highly-skilled, technical, administrative and managerial positions in the industrialised home countries. Except for female clerical staff, most white-collar and administrative positions in the developing country locations - of which there are few - are occupied by men, even in enterprises that employ mainly women. Those on the production line can look forward to seniority wage increments, but not to a change of job. A few may rise through the ranks to more highly-skilled posts, such as line-leader, quality inspector or even supervisor. But only few make the jump to technical or white-collar positions from the factory floor. The situation of women in the same industries in industrialised countries is, however, not very different in this respect.(Green, 1983, p.304).

Internal job ladders are short, and are blocked at the upper levels by women's lack of educational and technical qualifications, and also at times by sex discrimination. Everything else being equal, a woman is less likely to be promoted than a man (Wong, 1983). This is partly because of prevailing sex stereotypes and prejudices in society at large and the persistence of custom and tradition. But some companies also deliberately prefer men in supervisory positions, because it maintains external social relations of female subordination to male authority, and thus serves to enhance discipline in the factory.

Performance and seniority are the most important criteria for promotion, and workers who join a new company early have the best opportunities for promotion (USAID, 1981). Because of the youth and short work-life of the female workforce, latecomers are at a disadvantage - but less so that in male-dominated industries, given the generally higher turnover rates among women workers. More important, many women with seniority turn down offers of promotion - because they are content with their job, do not relish an increase in responsibility, or do not wish to jeopardise their personal relationship with other women on the line who may be long-time friends (Salaff and Wong, 1983, p. 229). (The companionship of other women is an important reason why women work (see Chapter V on social and cultural impact).) This reluctance to accept promotion reflects also the greater importance to women of their reproductive role. Awareness of sex discrimination and lack of long-term commitment to industrial labour due to the primacy of their reproductive role may also discourage women from taking advantage of opportunities for training and skill upgrading.

Furthermore, industrial training courses to upgrade skills are rare. Employers may be unwilling to give workers leave to attend them, and workers themselves may not be able to afford to forgo earned income for the duration of such courses, even if they could afford to pay for the courses as such. Where workers do invest in further training or in formal academic education, it is usually after work hours. In Malaysia, for example, many factory women who are school failures and dropouts, and who cannot get better jobs, nevertheless aspire to white-collar and professional employment for which better paper qualifications are required. They thus work at re-taking examinations, although passing is difficult given part-time studying and the rigours of full-time work. In the Philippines and Thailand a good number of factory women are secondary school graduates who study for university entrance, while others are part-time undergraduates. And in Singapore women factory workers who enrol in the government-run, company-sponsored BEST (Better Education and Skills

Training) programme are motivated mainly to improve their English language skills so that they can obtain more desired service sector jobs such as those of salesgirls in big department stores, and in hotels and restaurants serving tourists and the English-speaking public. In all these cases, the aim of further training, subsidised by factory wages, is to provide mobility out of factory work altogether, towards more desired forms of employment.

Government policies and local labour market conditions do have an effect on skills training for women. In Singapore, for example, the Government has long encouraged women and girls to enter technical fields of training, such as electronics, but this has only been marginally successful. Most young girls who join Vocational and Industrial Training Board courses, for example, prefer "feminine" subjects such as beauty culture, hairdressing, clerical work, and food catering, although jobs in these fields are likely to pay less well than, for example, the job of electronics technician. This again reflects traditional feminine ideology and socialisation. Still, strong market demand has led to some increase in the numbers and proportions of women in technical occupations.

The Singapore Government has also established a Skills Development Fund which levies a payroll tax on employers that can only be recouped if they send employees for further training. So far most training funded by this scheme has been for managerial and administrative personnel, occasionally for clerical staff, and for technical personnel. Little has filtered down to the woman operator on the factory floor, largely because there are not really any positions to train her for that cannot be accomplished more quickly and cheaply with on-the-job training. Employers are also reluctant to release employees for training in a tight labour situation. This, for example, appears to be the fate of the textile training institute in Singapore - it cannot find enough students. Employers are also aware that most further training that they provide for employees only increases their mobility out of their current employment - compare, for example, the experience of the BEST programme mentioned above, two-thirds of whose participants are women, mainly factory workers.

It is frequently argued that most of the skills acquired on the factory floor, through in-plant training and experience on the job, are not transferable and therefore of little value to the worker's wider career development (Maex, 1983, p. 53). In most modern sector occupations, production operator skills are certainly not easily transferable, and workers may have to retrain or relearn new skills when they change jobs. Only the simplest and most general skills are fully transferable, e.g. physical lifting. Sewing skills learned on the job in garments factories are transferable, e.g. workers can take in seamstressing at home, or even set up their own tailoring shops if they are lucky and skilful. But it is doubtful if this yields them a higher income than so-called non-transferable skills learned in an electronics factory, where wages are much higher than can be earned in garments homework. In fact, some of the skills learned in electronics are transferable, enabling workers to move from factory to factory where the industry is large and experienced labour is in demand. On the other hand, in this and other "high-tech" industries employing mainly women, rapid technological change makes many skills quickly obsolete, and they can only be taught and learned continuously on the job. Thus "transferability" may often not be a very useful concept to be applied in assessing the values of skills acquired. For many workers, the use of factory income to enhance their formal education provides the main means for desired upward and outward mobility from factory employment - which is much more important to them than acquiring transferable industrial skills.

The fact that women generally have less education, fewer skills, and fewer training and promotion opportunities than men in industrial employment is only partly explained by explicit employer sex discrimination. Rather, the occupational structure of industries employing mainly women, and traditional role perceptions and practical constraints imposed by women's reproductive role and associated "feminine" interests, are primarily responsible. Favourable government policies and a favourable labour market situation can only partly and slowly correct this.

As for differences between multinationals and non-multinationals, this depends greatly on the industry and occupational structure of particular enterprises. Generally, on the one hand, multinationals may be expected to have fewer promotion opportunities for women because higher-level positions are more concentrated in the industrialised or home countries. On the other hand, since the technological level of multinationals is generally higher and they are on average larger than national enterprises, they may actually offer more promotion opportunities. The international division of labour also changes over time, even within a given multinational, in response to local country as well as international market and technological conditions. Thus, for example, more higher-level jobs have been transferred from the industrialised to the newly-industrialising countries over time. Cultural variables also play a part. Asian home-based multinational enterprises, for example, often seem to have more reserves against promoting women to higher-level positions, while, for instance, multinationals of the United States seem frequently more inclined to do so - a reflection of the different cultural conditions found in the respective home country societies.

Job satisfaction and assessment

There have been few studies of job satisfaction among women workers in multinational industrial enterprises in developing countries, and there are many methodological problems inherent in such research especially as regards the separation of factors which are specific to these enterprises. Some studies covering Guatemala, Malaysia and Singapore found that the majority of women in multinationals were in general satisfied with their jobs. The proportion reported in Guatemala was 95 per cent while in Singapore 63 per cent said they were either happy or very happy with their job - the major reason for job dissatisfaction was low wages.[37] At the same time factory work whether in multinational or other companies is not seen as ideal even by satisfied workers, who would prefer other kinds of work, mainly white-collar work. One study found that 46 per cent of women factory workers in Malaysia wished to change their jobs, but only 7 per cent of workers in the same multi-national in Thailand (Blake, 1984). A study on Singapore found that 43 per cent of multinational electronics workers would prefer another kind of job, and only 57 per cent wished to remain in factory labour.

The problem is that for most workers these higher job aspirations are not realistic, given their own qualifications and the state of the local labour market. However, factory work is clearly preferred over all realistic options. A few quotes relating to various country situations illustrate this:

> A factory job in Brazil and Latin America generally, represents a considerable advancement over jobs in the informal sector. Brazil (Safa, 1983, p. 99).

> The consensus is that maquiladora work offers the best employment alternative in Cuidad Juarez. Mexico (Fernandez-Kelly, 1983, p. 217).

> Although the work was dull, extremely fatiguing on the eyes, and poorly paid, employment was highly valued, both because of the regular income and the many social contacts at work. Curacao (Abraham-Van der Mark, 1983, p. 381).

> There is no doubt that many of the girls regard working in the factories as better than the alternative work available to them, whether this be domestic work in their own homes or as servants in other people's homes. Indonesia (Mather, 1982).

> Factory work is accorded considerable prestige relative to such occupations as domestic servant and rubber tapper ... The regular wages and hours of factory work are preferred to small-scale self-employment, such as selling cooked food or tailoring. Factory work is regarded as "clean", "light" and secure indoor work suited to young women. Malaysia (Ackerman, 1984).

The wages and benefits are good relative to other work alternatives for young women with this educational background. Because production does not require heavy manual labour and takes place in clean air-conditioned surroundings, the job is considered by workers to be almost as good as white-collar work. Thailand (Blake, 1984).

For most women working in multinational factories, their jobs are a superior and welcome alternative to other female occupations available including the sometimes likely alternative of prostitution and destitution. It has been found for instance that in Morocco abandoned and destitute women now have the means of financial independence through wage employment. Women in intolerable marriages may also now be able to break out of them, which was previously impossible (Joekes, 1982, p. 75). In Malaysia it has been observed that economic independence has saved many women from falling into disreputable occupations as prostitutes, bar hostesses, or masseuses. In the past also many Malay women who were divorced, widowed or poor had few occupations to turn to, but now the availability of steady incomes from industrial employment and the opportunity to upgrade skills have tended to change this (Tan, 1984).

In relative terms, then, women evaluate their multinational factory jobs positively, although some may still be dissatisfied with their inability to obtain better jobs, which is a function of qualifications and job availability, i.e. the state of the local labour market. The level of satisfaction or dissatisfaction depends on the particular situation. In Singapore, for example, factory work ranks relatively low on the job hierarchy, but in Thailand it ranks quite high. Thus workers in Thailand are more satisfied with their jobs though their real wages and working conditions are inferior to those obtaining in Singapore for the same work (which has attracted many Thai women to work as foreign workers in Singapore electronics factories). Ultimately it is not so much the superiority of multinational employment which causes this positive evaluation but rather the inferiority of existing local alternatives for women.

Industrial relations aspects

A major concern about women's employment in multinationals in developing countries has been their degree of union organisation (Fuentes and Ehrenreich, 1983 and Ford 1983). One cause of this perceived low rate of unionisation could be the restrictive labour legislation of some host governments to attract multinational investment in manufacturing for export. These labour restrictions consist, amongst others, in limiting the workers' right to organise, to bargain and to strike (Dror, 1984). A study of Malaysia, the Philippines and Singapore showed that among the inducements to foreign investors in Malaysia the Industrial Relations Act forbade unions to bargain over terminations due to redundancy or reorganisation within the undertaking. Workers were prevented from holding union office unless they had been working for at least three years, and "pioneer industries" were exempted for five years from collective labour agreements with terms and conditions of employment more favourable than those stipulated by law (Blake, 1984). In Singapore the Industrial Relations Act did not permit bargaining over benefits such as annual leave and sick leave. And in the Philippines the Government had suspended the right to strike in vital industries, which undermined the bargaining power of the unions (Kassalow, 1978). In the export processing zone of the Republic of Liberia no strikes are permitted unless several procedures for amicable settlement and mediation have been followed and the union has permission through the Courts of Liberia (Botchie, 1984).

Multinationals themselves are sometimes allegedly opposed to trade unions, and are even said to leave a location if unions become too powerful. Some multinationals which have avoided unionisation in their home country, have tried to carry out the same policy in Malaysia. In Singapore, on the other hand, where several multinationals tried to negotiate a "no union" condition, the Singapore Economic Development Board refused, and one multinational finally accepted unionisation (Kassalow, 1978).

But in fact there appears to be no correlation between restrictive labour legislation or unionisation and attractiveness for foreign investments. Some countries with a rather restrictive labour legislation have been unsuccessful in attracting multinational investment while other countries which are more liberal towards labour have been more successful. There are indeed indications that multinationals may prefer to locate in countries with a more liberal labour legislation as they are more likely to be politically stable in the long run (Lim, 1983, pp. 76-77). The initiative for the restriction of the rights of the workers where it exists normally comes from the governments, rather than from the multinationals themselves. So, apart from the more important human rights' dimension, a restrictive policy towards labour seems to be irrelevant for attracting foreign investments.

There are great differences in unionisation rates by country and by industry. Around 1980, the proportion unionised was 7 per cent in the Republic of Korea, 17 per cent in Malaysia, 8 per cent in the Philippines, 24 per cent in Singapore, and 5 per cent in Thailand. For Hong Kong this figure was 18 per cent (Deyo, 1984; Blake, 1984; Multinational Monitor, 1983). The figure for the Republic of Korea represents an increase since 1960, for Singapore it represents a decline and for Hong Kong no change. Given the rapid growth of the labour force, the absolute number of unionised workers has increased.

The proportion of unionised workers is higher for wage earners than for the workforce as a whole, and highest in manufacturing.

Thus it is not surprising that there is a greater degree of unionisation among female factory workers in these countries than among the female wage-earning labour force as a whole. One report estimated that 30 per cent of factory women in the Republic of Korea, 50 per cent in Singapore, and 80 per cent of female textile workers in Thailand were unionised in 1979 (Yoon, 1979, p. 34). A study of the electronics industry in Singapore reports that 40 to 45 per cent of its mostly female labour force is unionised, compared to only 30 per cent in all manufacturing (Wong, 1983, p. 20). Because of the prominence of this industry, which employs mainly women and is dominated by multinationals, 60 per cent of all unionised workers in this sector are women. The high proportion of unionised workers in Singapore reflects both its high level of urbanisation and industrialisation.

There are also significant differences in unionisation rates by industry, though these too vary by country. For example, the textile and garments industry is usually more heavily unionised than the electronics industry, because it has been established much longer, and has a much longer union tradition. Electronics is a new, young industry, and usually has not been sufficiently established for organisation to take hold. Singapore is an exception, but there the industry has been established for nearly 20 years. In some cases the electronics industry is more heavily unionised in the developing than in the industrialised countries. The electronics industry in the United States, for example, has very low unionisation rates, especially in newer locations, and some multinationals from the United States which do not have unions in their home plants do have them in their plants in developing countries (Green, 1983, p. 286).

As far as women are concerned, it is multinationals in export-oriented industries like garments and electronics which have paved the way for their unionisation. These industries concentrate large numbers of women workers together in large enterprises for the first time, rather than in family, cottage and small-scale enterprises in which they were previously employed. For the first time in these countries, there is the opportunity for women to organise in predominantly female unions, led by women.

In Thailand for example, the industries in which women are most active are those dominated by multinationals, and they are taking leadership roles in the textile, electronics and stationery industries. Also in the Philippines, there are big unions with women workers, particularly in garments and electronics (Christian Conference of Asia, 1981b, p. 96).

Most studies show that multinational enterprises, not only those employing mainly women, are more likely to be unionised than national enterprises. This is true for example in the Philippines, Singapore and Thailand (Ramos, 1976, p. 73; Jurado, 1979, p. 5; Christian Conference of Asia, 1981b, p. 18; Pang and Lim, 1977, p. 29).

Among the reasons are the larger size of the multinationals, the somewhat better-educated labour force they tend to employ and the fact that they are often used to unions in their home plants in the industrialised countries (although this is not necessarily true for the United States). It is easier to organise workers who are working in large groups together, than workers who are scattered over the country in small enterprises, as the example of women shows. Moreover, small local enterprises often have less experience with unions, and are used to paternalistic relations between owner-managers and workers.

The managers of multinational enterprises bring the management style of their home countries with them, like, for instance, job evaluation systems and methods of wage determination. Many developing countries have adopted a policy of reducing the number of expatriate employees in multinational subsidiaries. However, the experience in Malaysia, the Philippines and Singapore shows that the local incumbent does not always inherit all the responsibilities of his expatriate predecessor. Indigenisation can have negative effects for the workers as in some cases the headquarters tend to centralise the decision-making after a national has replaced the expatriate manager, which makes bargaining for the unions more difficult (Kassalow, 1978, p. 283).

In export processing zones,[38] low rates of unionisation may be traced to the newness of the industries, to the physical isolation from supportive working class communities with a stronger tradition of union activity, to the migrant characteristics of workers who do not have strong ties with each other, and in some cases to associated government legislation which, while not always directly aimed at zone industries, affects them disproportionately because of their youth and the predominance of enterprises (both national and multinational) receiving government investment incentives.

In fact, some multinationals in certain countries seem deliberately to have avoided locating in export processing zones because of the risk of labour unrest where union rights were restricted, and because the physical construction of the zones (namely limited entry and exit points) makes it easy for workers to set up pickets that can affect all enterprises in the zones. The large strikes of women workers, including sympathy strikes, in the Bataan Export Processing Zone in recent years bear this out, and there have been similar incidents elsewhere, e.g. in the Bayan Lepas Free Trade Zone in Malaysia (Christian Conference of Asia, 1981b, pp. 28-33).

In Indonesia industrial action in the female-dominated textile and garments industry is undertaken precisely to press for unionisation. Unions would streamline the labour relations situation, and probably have a stabilising effect. Incidents of strikes and other labour action in factories employing mainly women (not necessarily multinationals) in developing countries do not, however, contradict the general picture of labour peace in most multinational enterprises. For example, work stoppages have declined over the years in Hong Kong, the Republic of Korea and Singapore, even without an increase in labour controls, as industrialisation and multinational employment have spread. This is probably because export-oriented industrialisation in these places has been a success, high employment has been achieved, and workers' incomes and job security have improved over the years, i.e. there is less labour discontent. Multinationals are perhaps less likely to experience labour unrest than national enterprises to the extent that they generally pay higher wages, provide better benefits and have better conditions than the average national enterprise. They usually observe government legislation and regulations to which they sometimes give particular attention because of political sensitivity towards foreign companies. In the Philippines, for example, one study found that while 62 per cent of multinationals were unionised, less than 4 per cent of these reported labour unrest, far less than in non-unionised, non-multinational enterprises (Jurado, 1979). Another study reported that the trade unions also prefer the relatively formal procedures for the settlement of disputes to more informal "family-style" approaches of some local enterprises (Kassalow, 1978, p. 283). However, there are exceptions to this trend. Thus, in Thailand, among the urban female wage-labour force it is the well-paid employees of multinationals who are said to be the most likely to strike (Tongudai, 1984).

In summary, it would appear that women working for multinational industrial enterprises are likely to be more unionised than women in other wage-jobs, and are in some cases even more unionised than male wage earners. They may even be more heavily unionised than women working for these same enterprises and industries in the industrialised countries. Multinational industrial enterprises are also much more likely to be unionised than non-multinationals in many developing countries. Young women have been active in labour unions and actions and have generally proved themselves to be less docile than was once imagined. Their participation in union activities is still low, but in most countries it has been increasing over time as their industries and their own employment have become more established. At the same time it is not multinational employers who primarily determine the outcome of industrial relations, but rather a host of locally-specific country factors. In many developing countries it seems easier to unionise and bargain with multinational factories than with local factories, and multinationals often experience less labour unrest.

Employment security and job tenure

Recent layoffs in the developing countries due to the decline in the world economy, were in general fewer and of shorter duration than in the 1974-75 recession. Whether they occurred at all depended to some extent on the state of the local labour market. In Singapore's tight labour market, for example, employers hoarded labour during the recession for fear that they would not be able to rehire in the upturn. Lay-offs traceable to cyclical factors were also milder in the rapidly-growing electronics industry than in other industries.

The "footloose" or "runaway" behaviour sometimes assumed for multinationals has also so far proved to be more the exception than the rule, and an exception explained more readily by factors other than the expiry of tax holidays and the desire to escape to even lower wage costs elsewhere. The reasons for the handful of examples of major multinational shutdowns and relocations in developing countries would appear rather to include the following: failure of the parent company or a particular division or product-line; corporate takeover or reorganisation of the parent company; extreme political and/or economic (especially financial) instability in the host country; moving to a different location within the host country; persistent union problems and labour unrest; and loss of trade preferences to foreign markets.[39] In some cases, companies which closed had been operating for as long as 15 years.

However, the vast majority of multinational industrial enterprises in developing countries have remained and continue to remain in their locations despite expiring tax holidays, rising wages, increased unionisation, market and technological changes, and political and economic upheavals. Some have stayed on even when their operations have been persistently loss-making.[40] This is because the costs and risks of relocation, particularly constant relocation, are substantial for most multinationals. Smaller multinationals with less fixed investments are more likely to be mobile than others including some of the smaller enterprises from newly-industrialising countries which sometimes operate on narrow margins and are sensitive to small changes in local costs.

Technological change and increased protection of markets in the industrialised countries are likely to slow down the growth of new multinational export-oriented industrial employment in the developing world in general, but not to eliminate or reverse it on the whole. The distribution of such employment among developing countries may change. But in most of the countries which currently host large volumes of multinational investment and employment in export-oriented industry, particularly the newly-industrialising countries of Asia, the trend towards increasing female employment is unlikely to be abated.[41]

Cyclical lay-offs and permanent shutdowns aside, multinationals, as mentioned before, have been accused sometimes of encouraging labour turnover in their plants in order to keep wage costs low and/or to forestall unionisation (Ong, 1983, p. 431), for instance, by keeping workers on prolonged temporary status so that they can be easily fired at any time;[42] or by requiring women to resign on marriage although this may be against the law. Cases have been reported of workers being laid off on the pretext of market slowdown, only to be rehired sometimes in larger numbers a few months or even a few weeks later.[43]

Although such practices may occur among multinationals as among local enterprises, they usually reflect a more complex reality. It is by no means universal, or even usual, for multinationals to favour and to foster high rates of labour turnover. A certain amount of turnover is both inevitable (for workers' personal reasons, if nothing else) and functional, because it keeps the labour force flexible, but too much turnover raises recruitment costs and disrupts production and deliveries. It is particularly problematic in situations of labour shortage, but even in countries with surplus labour many employers prefer to stabilise employment to maintain an effective and reliable workforce.

Nor has it been demonstrated that women generally stay in factory employment for a shorter time than in alternative female occupations. On the other hand, a high proportion of workers on temporary, apprentice or probationary status (Ong, 1983, p. 432) is only to be expected in recently-established or rapidly-growing enterprises in which new workers form a large proportion of the workforce. This does not, however, invalidate the observation that some companies (not necessarily multinationals) operate a system of employing "permanent casual" labour (Jurado, 1979).

The average job tenure of women factory workers in multinationals varies from country to country and from time to time. In Mexico, the typical maquiladora worker stays in her job for an average of three years (Fernandez-Kelly, 1983, p. 214). In Malaysia, one study reported an average working life of three to four years (Ong, 1983, p. 431). In Hong Kong, Morocco and Singapore, many women work for ten or more years.[44] The average length of working life is shorter where industries and female factory employment are only recently established, and longer where they have been established longer. The tendency is for the average job tenure (itself shorter than the total working-life since many workers change jobs many times during their working-life) to increase over time.

Job tenure of women is often linked to the need to earn an income during periods where family income is insufficient. But absolute economic need for bare subsistence is not everywhere a predominant criterion determining women's length of working life. In Singapore, for example, women factory workers have continued to work, despite relatively high and secure incomes for both men and women, in order to enhance family living standards and the opportunities available to the next generation. The reduction of family size (to an average of two to three children per couple) has had an encouraging effect on female labour force participation, while the replacement of the extended family by the nuclear family has had a discouraging effect. High seniority wages also increase the opportunity cost of quitting the workforce. More recently, however, there are indications that, despite the exhortations, pleas and incentives of the government and employers, increasing numbers of married working-class women, including multinational factory workers, have been withdrawing from the workforce in favour of concentrating on their reproductive role.[45]

As for short-term labour turnover, there are many situations where this is lower for women than for men, given their greater economic need, fewer alternative employment opportunities, and lesser mobility.[46] Still, turnover is often lower among women multinational factory workers than other women workers.[47]

In sum, it appears that multinational factory employment for women in developing countries is not necessarily more unstable, insecure or short-lived than other forms of employment, particularly in local enterprises. The duration of employment varies from country to country and from time to time, and tends to lengthen over time in any one country. Women do have a shorter work-life than men, but this is more often the result of "voluntary" retirement at marriage than of involuntary lay-offs. It reflects to a large degree indigenous cultural values and social and economic structures, particularly the traditional sexual division of labour and the primacy of women's reproductive role. Female commitment to the labour force varies from situation to situation, by individual as well as by country, and appears to increase over time as women become more integrated in modern employment.

Notes

[1] For example, there are no export-processing zones in the free areas of Hong Kong and Singapore where much of multinational export manufacturing is located; and most multinational export manufacturing in countries like Indonesia, the Philippines and Thailand takes place outside such zones even where they exist. Malaysia is probably the only larger developing country where most multinational export manufacturing takes place in export processing zones. For an analysis of multinational enterprises employment in export-processing zones, see ILO (1981), Chapter 4, and Maex (1983).

[2] This takes account of the fact that total world-wide employment in export-processing zones in developing countries is supposed to be in the region of 1 million. Some 80 per cent of this is estimated to be in textile/garments and electronics where women constitute some 75 per cent of the labour force (600,000 women). Assuming for the rest of the export-processing zone industries the average female participation rate of 30 per cent, total employment of women in export-processing zones would amount to about 660,000. Approximately

60 per cent of these (or 400,000) are supposed to be in multinationals (elements for these estimates have been derived from Maex (1983)). According to Fernandez-Kelly (1983b) women account for between 75 and 90 per cent of those working in export processing zones, so that the above-mentioned estimate would be low rather than high.

[3] Vertical integration and the international division of labour within the multinational corporation generally concentrate higher-level jobs in developed countries.

[4] See Maex (1983), pp. 49-52, for a recent summary of sources. See also the various country case studies cited in the references, e.g. studies by Christian Conference of Asia, Fernandez-Kelly, Jamilah, Lim, Wong, and others.

[5] That is to say, peak labour productivity is reached early, so that after a certain point - several months or a year at most - more experienced workers are not more productive than workers with less experience, yet are more costly due to the practice of seniority wage increases. See, for example, Lim (1978b).

[6] Joekes (1982), United States Agency for International Development (1981), Abraham-Van der Mark (1983), Bolles (1984), Hein (1981), Standing (1978).

[7] For example, Lim (1978b), Grossman (1979), Elson and Pearson (1981), Safa (1981), Ong (1983) and others.

[8] Smith (1982). The retirement age for women in the companies concerned has been reported to remain lower than that of men (45 rather than the standard 55 years of age).

[9] Jurado (1979), Perpinan (no date), Villegas (1978) and others on the Philippines.

[10] See, for example, Grossman (1979), Frobel, Heinrichs and Kreye (1980), Ong (1983).

[11] Ackerman (1979 and 1984) and Jamilah (1980, 1981a, 1981b, 1982 and 1984).

[12] Wages in jobs such as salesgirl in Singapore may not be better paid than factory labour but working conditions and status are generally higher.

[13] The ratio of applicants per job in countries like Thailand and the Philippines is often as high as five or ten to one.

[14] Pang and Lim (1982). An earlier (1975) study of one textile factory found that 80 per cent of the female workers were Malaysian migrants. See Heyzer (1982).

[15] Bustamente (1983), p. 252, Joekes (1982), Yoon (1979), p. 17, Christian Conference of Asia (1981b), p. 104, and Zuhairah (1983), p. 192.

[16] For example, new workers recruited by friends and relatives receive considerable moral support and subtly coercive social pressure from them to stay in the job as fulfilment of their obligation for the favour rendered. Also, workers with personal ties at the workplace are likely to be more content and settled and less likely to "job-hop" in search of a more satisfactory situation. On the other hand, there is also the very real risk that workers who quit may take their friends and relatives with them.

[17] Heyzer (1982), p. 180, Berlin (1983), p. 265. Singapore recruiters often rely on local agents, e.g. in Thailand.

[18] Christian Conference of Asia (1981b), p. 104.

[19] See in this connection motives advanced for multinationals in a very labour-intensive sector in the study on Social and labour practices of multinational enterprises in the textiles, clothing and footwear industries (Geneva, ILO, 1984), pp. 51-52.

[20] For example, in the Philippines the minimum wage for the Bataan Export Processing Zone is lower than that for the Metro Manila area; in Thailand, the minimum wage for Bangkok was until recently higher than for the provincial city of Chiegmai; in Indonesia, the minimum wage is higher in Jakarta than in outlying regions; in Malaysia the market wage is lower in rural than in urban export-processing zones.

[21] For example, some multinationals in south-east Asia have been known to pay their workers the highest wages in the industry to forestall unionisation (Edgren, 1982, p. 16).

[22] For a discussion of wage-payment systems in large manufacturing companies employing mainly women in Malaysia, see Thong (1983).

[23] Many employers admit adjusting targets to permit only a predetermined percentage - usually 10 per cent to 25 per cent - of the workers to earn the incentive bonus.

[24] In Singapore, for example, new high-technology companies have been unable to attract women workers away from established garment factories because experienced and skilful workers are able to earn very high wages through the piece-rate system.

[25] For example, in Singapore a woman worker with ten years' seniority in a multinational electronics factory can earn as much as a recent university graduate.

[26] Fernandez-Kelly (1983), Aguiar (1983), Christian Conference of Asia (1981b), Subido (1979), Salaff and Wong (1983). See also ILO (1976).

[27] Christian Conference of Asia (1981b), Tongudai (1984).

[28] There is a high failure rate in small-scale commercial activities and market trading traditionally dominated by women.

[29] This seems true in other sectors of the economy as well. See, for example, Christian Conference of Asia (1984), pp. 31-32 and 62.

[30] Twenty-six per cent of the electronics companies had industrial clinics on factory premises, staffed by industrial nurses and visited by company-appointed doctors for a few hours each day - other companies had workers leave the premises to seek treatment from company-appointed panels of doctors.

[31] Wong (1983), Salaff and Wong (1983) and Far Eastern Economic Review, 21 June 1984.

[32] In Malaysia, Thong (1983).

[33] For example, in the Republic of Korea, the mother of a new-born child must be given two 30-minute breaks per working day for child care. Kyu (1979).

[34] Maex (1983), p. 57; Christian Conference of Asia (1981b), p. 11; Multinational Monitor (1983), p. 12.

[35] For the Republic of Korea, see Multinational Monitor (1983).

[36] See, for example, Green (1983), p. 307; Abraham-Van der Mark (1983), p. 381; Ong (1983), pp. 430-431; Perpinan (no date); Fuentes and Ehrenreich (1983), p. 31, etc.

[37] Zuhairah (1983); USAID (1981); Wong (1983).

[38] The ILO's Committee of Experts on the Application of Conventions and Recommendations has been considering the effect on ratified Conventions of the creation of export processing zones since 1981. See in particular ILO: Report of the Committee of Experts on the Application of Conventions and Recommendations, Report III (Part 4A), International Labour Conference, 70th Session, Geneva, 1984, pp. 12-15, especially para. 38.

[39] For examples of multinational plant closures in various countries see Aguira(1983), pp. 133-134 (Brazil); Bolles (1983), p. 144 (Jamaica); Abraham-Van der Mark (1983), pp. 381-382 (Curacao); Perpinan (no date), p. 5 (Philippines); Robbins and Siegel (1980) (Mexico, Hong Kong); Multinational Monitor (1983), pp. 12, 22 (Republic of Korea).

[40] For example, the Ford Motor Company, one of the highest-paying and unionised multinationals in the Philippines, closed its car plants there only in 1984, after 14 years of making huge losses.

[41] See Lim (1984b), Lim (1984c), Lim (1984e), Lim (1985b).

[42] Perpinan (no date), p. 8, Paglaban (1978), p. 19, Jurado (1979), (Philippines); Fuentes and Ehrenreich (1983), p. 31 (Mexico); Christian Conference of Asia (1981b), pp. 10-11 (Thailand); Mather (1982) (Indonesia); etc.

[43] Christian Conference of Asia (1981b), p. 50 (Malaysia), p. 104 (Sri Lanka).

[44] Joekes (1982), p. 63; Salaff and Wong (1983), p. 225; Salaff (1981).

[45] The reasons are complex but for many women in Singapore withdrawal from the workforce is a rational allocation of their time and of family effort, rather than merely a reflection of traditional cultural values.

⁴⁶ For example, Joekes (1982) (Morocco); Hein (1981) (Mauritius); Standing (1978) (Jamaica).

⁴⁷ For example, a Philippine regional study found that women multinational factory workers had lower rates of turnover than female domestic servants and workers in small-scale local commercial enterprises (Costello (1984)).

CHAPTER V

WOMEN'S EMPLOYMENT IN MULTINATIONAL ENTERPRISES IN THE SERVICE SECTOR

Introduction

As has been pointed out in Chapter II (table 1), 19 per cent of the women's labour force in Africa in 1980 was employed in the service sector. The corresponding figures for Asia and Latin America were 13 and 69 per cent respectively. Taking these regions together, this means that of the total women's labour force in developing countries, about 17 per cent is employed in the service sector (Hopkins, 1983).

Of total employment (male and female) in the service sector, the share of women is 37 per cent in Africa, 24 per cent in Asia and 39 per cent in Latin America. Taking these regions together, the share of women was 27 per cent.

There are hardly any statistics available about the employment of women in multinationals in the service sector. According to a special ILO survey (ILO, 1980), no more than 9 per cent of total multinational employment in developing countries is in the service sector. This would mean an employment volume of about 350,000 people (1980); and if we assume that the rate of female employment in multinationals in the service sector is not different from that of the total service sector average, then about 94,500 women (corresponding to some 0.1 per cent of total female employment in the service sector in developing countries) are to be found in multinationals in this sector.

Financial and commercial services

Multinational enterprises' involvement in commercial and financial services in developing countries originated in the colonial era to serve other enterprises, many of them also multinationals, mostly engaged in international trade. Banks are the most prominent of these service sector multinationals, and are found even in those countries - mostly in Africa - where in comparison with other regions there are few other multinationals. Transportation companies, mainly shipping lines, and the famous import and export agency houses, were and are also important, particularly in export-oriented economies.

Until recently, service multinationals employed mainly men in the developing countries who were more likely than women to have attained the level of formal education (usually in the language of the ex-metropolitan country) necessary for employment in white-collar clerical, professional and managerial positions. The absolute numbers of workers in service multinationals of either sex employed were and are small, and they tend to form an élite within the labour force of developing countries, receiving much higher incomes and better fringe benefits than other workers. Since these are "modern" enterprises employing an educated labour force, they tend to adhere by all government labour legislation and regulations, and generally match or surpass conditions of employment in similar jobs elsewhere in the public and private sectors. Hours of work for most workers are regular "office hours", and working conditions are of good standard.

With the spread of female education, more women have begun to penetrate most levels of employment in these service multinationals, but they are still concentrated mainly in the lower-level clerical jobs. In most countries equal opportunities and terms and conditions of employment for men and women in these enterprises seem to exist, not only in the newly-industrialising countries.[1] But the general absence of women in higher-level jobs suggests that a certain amount of discrimination exists in hiring and promotions practices.

In only a very few developing countries are multinationals in the commercial and financial services sector large enough to account for a significant proportion of the female labour force. The most notable cases are the service centres of Hong Kong and Singapore, where home-based as well as foreign multinationals are also large employers in this sector.

The experience of the banking and financial services industry in Singapore may be particularly instructive. In the colonial period, which extended up to 1963, men dominated all levels of employment, including clerical positions, in this sector. In the 1960s and 1970s, the rapid expansion of education for women, and of jobs for both men and women in all sectors of the economy, including the fast-growing financial sector itself, led to a dramatic change in the sex ratio of employment. Women as a percentage of all workers in the financial and business services sector increased from 22 per cent in 1970 to 48 per cent in 1982 - the highest proportion of women in any sector (followed by manufacturing with 43 per cent women workers), and much higher than the national percentage of 36 per cent. Women as a percentage of clerical workers - the largest number of workers in this sector - increased from 31 per cent in 1970 to 64 per cent in 1982.[2] Elsewhere the share of women in employment in the financial and business services sector is: Hong Kong 40 per cent, the Republic of Korea 28 per cent, Indonesia 15 per cent and Iran 9 per cent. For Egypt the figure is 16 per cent and for some Latin American countries: Brazil 56 per cent, Venezuela 38 per cent and Peru 24 per cent.[3]

Most of the financial institutions in Singapore, whether foreign or home-based, are multinational in their operations. But foreign multinationals had a particular impact on the employment of women especially in the professional ranks of the labour force. When foreign banks came to Singapore in large numbers in the early 1970s, their demand for professional staff could not be met from the available supply of qualified males, particularly as most male university graduates were temporarily withdrawn from the labour market into the newly-introduced full-time military service. The foreign banks - especially from the United States - thus hired qualified women for professional and executive positions - a phenomenon rare in the traditionally male-dominated field of banking and finance anywhere. Through seniority and good performance, women maintained their hold on professional and executive jobs in this sector, and new jobs continued to be filled with a high proportion of women university graduates. However, by the late 1970s a backlash had emerged, with the banking community restricting its hiring of women, since the supply of male graduates had increased by this time. But compared to most other countries women remain well represented in the higher echelons of the labour force.

At least in this, and in other Asian cases, foreign multinationals especially appear to be more willing to employ women in professional and executive positions than other firms. But this in part may simply reflect the relative demand and supply of qualified labour for the sector. Where demand is strong and a supply of qualified female labour exists, it is likely to be employed. Foreign multinational banks may employ a higher proportion of women officers simply because they were established more recently when a greater supply of qualified women existed.

In other business and professional services where multinationals - including home-based multinationals in the developing countries - are being established (e.g. architectural, engineering, management and financial consultancy services), women with the necessary qualifications are readily employed when people with such qualifications are scarce overall. Education - especially university education - is the most important means by which a few women in developing countries can hurdle discriminatory sex barriers to high-level professional and managerial employment. Even then, however, some discrimination would seem to exist, especially with respect to promotions, since it is frequently assumed that women's first responsibility is to their families and that they will thus be unwilling or unable to assume higher responsibilities, with business travel, sometimes long and irregular hours, entertaining male clients, etc., essential in many top positions.[4]

Wholesale and retail services in most developing countries rarely involve direct employment by multinationals. One exception is the growing establishment of branches of large department stores and supermarkets from Japan in the affluent urban markets of south-east Asia like Hong Kong, Malaysia and Singapore. Such enterprises employ mostly women in sales and clerical positions.

Indirect employment by multinationals, however, always exists and appears to be growing. Examples include local distributors and agents for foreign companies, and locally-owned franchises of multinational chains, most notably fast-food chains from the United States which are flourishing in most south-east Asian and some Latin American countries, and which themselves employ a good proportion of women. In both cases, the sex distribution and terms and conditions of employment generally conform to local norms. But much also depends on the general state of the local labour market. In Singapore, for example, some newly established Japanese stores are raising the market wage for female sales staff. Fast-food outlets have begun to employ part-time youth and student labour as they do in the United States - not as a direct transfer of management practices from the United States or to undercut labour costs, but simply as another response to the labour market conditions.

Tourism and related personal services

The tourist industry in many developing countries is an important employer of women - as hotel chambermaids, restaurant waitresses, salesgirls, workers in travel agencies and airlines; especially in Asian countries like the Republic of Korea, the Philippines and Thailand, as social escorts; and, rarely, in management.

International hotel chains may be considered to be employing women indirectly as the hotels are often owned by locals and operated under management contracts with the international chains. Others are joint ventures between local entrepreneurs and the foreign hotel chains. Actually, relatively few of these hotels are directly or wholly owned by foreign multinationals. Tourist-related jobs are, however, not exclusively or even mostly filled by women. Much depends again on the state of the local labour market: where there is high unemployment and male wages are low, male and female workers are employed interchangeably in these labour-intensive service jobs.

Many of the larger (and frequently multinational) hotels in developing countries are unionised, and terms and conditions of employment are therefore better than in similar jobs in non-unionised enterprises. The work environment especially in the big hotels - air-conditioned, luxurious - may be considered relatively pleasant, and perquisites such as subsidised food, and tips from guests and customers, which enhance real income, are not uncommon. But the situation varies according to local conditions, and even by employer in a given country. One report from the Philippines complains about intimidation and non-recognition of the union in a number of large international chain hotels in Manila. Yet the workers are organised and affiliated to a union movement. There are also complaints of being paid only the minimum wage for years, but because of tips and service charges the hotel workers usually take home more than skilled workers in other industries. The income is thus felt to be just enough to support workers' families, which are typically large (Lee, 1981).

Notes

[1] For example, communication received from Ministry of Labour, Uganda.

[2] Lim (1982) and Ministry of Labour, Singapore: Report of the Labour Force Survey of Singapore 1982.

[3] Calculated from ILO: Yearbook of Labour Statistics 1983, (Geneva).

[4] See, for example, Lim (1982).

CHAPTER VI

SOCIOLOGICAL IMPACT OF MNEs ON WOMEN WORKERS
IN MANUFACTURING

Income, expenditure and living standards

Employment in multinational industrial enterprises significantly increases the incomes of women in developing countries, and their families. Workers who have previously held other jobs enjoy a considerable income gain, for example, of 30 per cent in Malaysia and 35 per cent in the Philippines (Maex, 1983, p. 55). But few receive a wage large enough to support the typical family even at poverty level; and this is the rule rather than the exception in many countries, even for male wage-workers.[1] Working-class families live by pooling the incomes of multiple income-earners. The incomes of women factory workers do substantially raise total family incomes, in most cases sufficiently to push them over the poverty level. In Hong Kong, for example, one study found that working daughters augmented their families' incomes by 30 per cent to 70 per cent (Salaff, 1981, p. 263).

It is not uncommon for the factory women, even those who are young and relatively new workers, to be the highest income-earners in their families, earning more than fathers, brothers and husbands. This, for example, has been reported for multinational electronics workers in Mexico, Singapore and Thailand.[2] In Morocco one study found that 32 per cent of the women factory workers (not all in multinationals) were the highest income-earners for their families (Joekes, 1982, p. 63). A significant proportion of the women workers in several countries are also sole earners for their households, and would be destitute if not for their factory jobs. Others are the only steady wage earners for their families, with other family members contributing only occasional irregular income from variable informal sector activities, casual labour and remittances from foreign countries.[3] Thus in many, if not most, countries women workers in multinational factories cannot be considered secondary income earners only for their families.

The biggest item of expenditure out of women factory workers' wages is the contribution to their families. The vast majority in all countries (about 85 per cent on average) do make such a contribution. A typical proportion is about one-half, more for those workers still living at home (see below), and only slightly less for those who are migrants living away from home. For example, one study in Mexico found that single women factory workers contribute on average more than one-half of their earnings to their families; another study in Venezuela found that they contributed more than one-half; a report from Hong Kong cites a figure as high as three-quarters of the wage; and a study in Singapore found that 49 per cent of the workers gave their families one-half of their wages while an additional 12 per cent gave all their wages.[4] Similar figures are reported for other countries.

The families themselves use the additional income in various ways which vary with family size, composition and life-cycle. When the dependency ratio is high (i.e. the family is young and large, including many young children, and there are few income-earners), the woman's wages are spent on the bare necessities of living, such as rent, food and basic clothing. When the dependency ratio drops and/or incomes increase, the money is spent on the younger children's education, and on the working daughters' own further education. Consumer durables (such as radios, refrigerators, sewing machines, telephones, televisions and sometimes washing machines, video recorders and chandeliers - especially in Singapore and Hong Kong), and finally improved housing, are other items of consumption once basic needs and education have been taken care of (Salaff, 1981). Among Chinese communities in Hong Kong and Singapore, expenditure on maintaining family kinship networks are also important; and in Singapore, contributions of the married women's income towards the purchase of public housing units (Salaff, 1981; Salaff and Wong, 1983).

The women do spend some of their wages on themselves. This depends on the size of the wage relative to individual and family living requirements, and on the family's economic status. For example, in Hong Kong, Malaysia, Sri Lanka and Tunisia[5] the woman's trousseau, dowry or other wedding-related expenses such as the wedding banquet, household goods and furniture, command a major proportion of their wages, even wages which have been handed over to the father or mother. Beyond saving for marriage, women workers in both Latin American and Asian countries spend their income on more fashionable (and modern) clothing and other personal items, small luxuries, gifts, and social activities with friends, such as shopping and film shows.[6]

In short, the expenditure patterns of women factory workers, including those in multinationals who are better-paid, reveal that their employment substantially increases their own and their families' living standards, especially over time as wages increase. The families become more economically secure, and are able to consume itmes, including items which contribute to their own upward mobility, such as education, which would otherwise be out of their reach. Women workers' contribution is often so significant that in localised communities there is a visible and appreciated difference between the prosperity and even the status of families with and without daughters working in nearby industrial enterprises. This has been found, for instance, for such workers employed in multinational factories in rural areas of Malaysia which are close to export processing zones (Ackerman, 1984).

Family relations

There are two main hypotheses about the impact that multinational factory employment as other industrial employment has on women's role and position in their families in developing countries. The first, "conservative", hypothesis is that women's, especially young women's, traditional position of subordination in the patriarchal family is unchanged, or even reinforced by their factory work experience - which itself is considered basically exploitative. The second, "progressive", hypothesis is that women's role and position in the family and in society changes, endowing them with greater power (or less powerlessness) as they become more independent and "modern" in outlook, self-perception and behaviour, including in relations with their families ("liberating" women on the one side but "disrupting" traditional role perception on the other).

In most developing, as in industrialised countries, women are subject to the authority of fathers, husbands, village heads and government leaders, all of whom are male, and must approve or at least permit, and may even encourage or direct, their working in industry. In some cases, village heads and government officials may even personally participate in industrial activities and benefit from multinational industrial investment, e.g. as partners in joint ventures, as higher-level employees, in keeping with traditional systems of patronage and patron-client obligations.[7] (These facts speak for the "conservative" hypothesis.)

But patriarchal authorities also often disapprove of or oppose women's employment in multinational factories. In some rural situations, such employment attracts women away from traditional occupations such as farm labour on family or tenant farms, thus raising rural wages or even causing labour shortages which adversely affect fathers and landlords. For example, in many areas of Malaysia, the employment of rural Malay women in manufacturing multinationals has resulted in the abandonment of rice-lands due to the shortage of labour. This lowers agricultural rents and land values and is not welcomed by rural landowners and even the women's own families in some cases (Siraj, 1984).

Fathers and village leaders may also be unwilling to share or surrender authority over their daughters with strangers, particularly foreign employers, and find it hard to accept their greater independence as a result of factory work. Many fathers also fear that their daughters' working reflects badly on their own ability to provide for their families. There may also be objection to single young women migrating and living alone in cities, working night shifts, and participating in "modern" social and cultural activities available in urban areas and/or fostered by companies. This has been noted to be a concern of Islamic authorities in Malaysia, for example (Siraj, 1984). Finally, fathers may not like their daughters working in the factories because of the possible social stigma and damage to their moral reputations (see the section on community relations below), but are forced to accede due to economic need. In other cases, fathers are actually absent, or the young women work in defiance of their objections.

A question which follows is whether women's increased contribution to family income changes their position within the family. In some situations, particularly of single young women living at home, they hand over their entire wages to the head of the family. Formally, this is usually (not always) the father. But practically, it is usually the mother who controls family finances and the daughter's wage. Thus the young woman's wage strengthens the position of the senior woman in the household.[8] In other cases, women hand over only a portion of their wage. But in most cases, they retain influence, sometimes considerable influence, over how that wage - even the portion which is turned over for the family's general use - is spent. Part of this reflects working daughters' higher level of education and greater experience of the modern world as a result of their employment. Less educated fathers and mothers may thus consult their older working daughters about their younger siblings' education or choice of jobs (Salaff, 1981).

There is little doubt therefore that in nearly all situations the working woman's status within the family is enhanced. She is more frequently accorded greater respect - even from members of the extended family. In the home, she is relieved of domestic chores, which are performed for her by her mother or non-working sisters. There is greater tolerance of "modern" behaviour on her part, such as dating and choosing her own marriage partner rather than having one chosen for her, and delaying the age of marriage. This is true even of an extremely conservative situation such as that in Pakistan (Weiss, 1983, p. 210). Even premarital pregnancy is often accepted by the family, especially in child-centered societies (Salaff, 1981). (These facts sustain the "progressive" hypothesis.)

Married women who work - an increasing proportion of the multinational factory labour force - also do so in consultation with their husbands. Again, because of economic need, there is rarely questioning of the woman's decision to work, and in many countries "husband's permission" becomes a less important factor over time, e.g. in Singapore (Salaff and Wong, 1983; Wong, 1982, 1983). Economic need itself may be defined less in absolute terms (i.e. survival) than in terms of the family's jointly decided rising aspirations for a better life, e.g. in Hong Kong and Singapore.[9] Even in patriarchal cultures, women frequently control disposition of the family income, and where they contribute to this income, their control is usually enhanced - at least partly because working outside the home itself gives them more information and experience in making financial decisions. In all such settings, joint husband-wife decision-making is the most common form of family decision-making and as women work their relative power and authority increase (Wong, 1982; Chiang, 1984). In some cases, the woman may even dominate family decision-making, including major financial decisions. Studies in the Philippines and Singapore have also found a tendency for men to share more in household duties, including child-raising, although women still bear the brunt of domestic responsibilities, and consequently work longer hours both within and outside the home than men do.[10]

Family relations are intrinsically important to women who work, no less than they are to those who do not. Migrant women workers, for example, not only faithfully send large remittances to their families, but also visit them frequently, and receive them as visitors. This is particularly common in Malaysia, where distances between migrants and their home villages are shorter than in many other countries (Heyzer, 1982; Zuhairah, 1983).

In general, it may be concluded that the strengthening of women's position within the family strengthens and democratises the family, attenuating cultural stereotypes with regard to age and sex, and even cements links with the wider extended family beyond the individual nuclear unit despite a continuing formal patriarchical structure and authority system. As the status of working women within the family improves, women may also become more desirable marriage partners (Ackerman, 1984).

Although factory employment may undermine male authority within the family, this effect is not necessarily culturally disruptive. Cultural disruption - for the men - is most likely to occur where men remain unemployed and must be dependent on women for income, though even this is not inevitable. For example, in the Caribbean, women have long been the major breadwinners (Abraham-Van der Mark, 1983; Bolles, 1983), while in Thailand women have traditionally had considerable responsibility for family economic support. In these situations it is not necessarily disruptive for women to earn more than men, or for men to earn nothing at all, especially if it is recognised that this is due to a weak male labour market rather than to individual failure. The situation in most developing countries today, however, is different from that in industrialised countries at a comparable stage of their economic development, in that employment for men may not be generated more rapidly than that for women. The influence of female earning power may thus be more common and potentially more disruptive of traditional male authority in developing countries today than was the case in the industrialised countries.

Whether or not women's employment in multinational factories has a culturally disruptive effect on family relations, multinationals per se seem to have little to do with it. The most important factor seems to be that multinational as other industrial enterprises provide modern sector wage employment, which takes women out of the home and gives them an income. But education, urbanisation, migration and the mass media also influence the structure of the family and family relations in more or less the same "modernising" directions. Multinationals as such at best have a marginal effect because of their higher wages and, to a lesser extent, their often more "modern" social relations within the factory.

Finally, the strengthening of women's position within the family does not come without some personal costs. For some unmarried women, family economic needs mean that they may actually have to postpone marriage longer than they desire, or to forego it altogether as their marriageability declines with age (Salaff, 1981). Others may dislike and suffer from factory work but feel compelled to remain in it, and to preserve their jobs, because of family responsibility. This may make them more resigned to their work situations and less likely to organise and press for improvements. In most situations the traditional sexual division of labour and its supporting ideology remain fairly intact. From a feminist point of view, women's factory employment may not in fact be sufficiently disruptive of traditional family relations to be truly "liberating" of women. Cultural disruption which has negative consequences for men and for male-dominated society may in fact have positive consequences for women. Thus both certain elements of the "conservative" and the "progressive" hypothesis on the effect of women's employment in modern industrial enterprises, including multinationals, are confirmed by the available evidence.

Community relations

Where the women are mostly local residents, for example, in large urban settings such as Bangkok and Singapore, the community experiences few changes as a result of their employment by multinationals, and most of these changes are positive, like the multiplier effect of increased local incomes. Most of the women are living at home with their parents or husbands, and do not make new demands on local housing, transportation or other social infrastructure. Factory employment is unlikely to introduce behavioural changes which might cause frictions with the community. Being urban residents, both the women and their neighbours have already been exposed to "modern" behaviour patterns among women.

On the other hand, where multinational enterprises introduce a large new population of migrant women workers into a small community - the situation in many export processing zones, for example - tensions and conflicts are likely to arise between the women workers and their host community. The women may exert pressure on limited local infrastructure, especially on housing and transportation facilities, and particularly in rural or semi-rural areas. Local landowners and shopkeepers may benefit, and the local families whose own daughters find factory jobs, but other working residents can be inconvenienced, for example from the rise in rents and other local costs of living from increased population pressure. Particularly in conservative rural communities, residents may resent the more modern behaviour patterns of the factory workers, and fear their influence on local young men and women. Unlike in a large urban setting where the women workers merely blend into a much larger population including other factory workers, in smaller urban, suburban and rural settings they will form a conspicuous group of strangers who might even outnumber local residents.

Explicit conflicts between women and their host communities, however, have been reported only in a few instances, for example, in Malaysia, where a large proportion of workers in export processing zones are migrants, especially from Malay villages. Some of the conflicts were economic in nature. For example, local residents blamed the workers for local inflation, while the workers were resentful of local residents for overcharging them for housing and other essential goods (Blake, 1975, 1984).

But the major issue of contention observed appears to be workers' "moral behaviour". Traditional local residents object to the young women living alone, out of the authority and control of male family members, socialising with men outside the local community (Blake, 1980).

Although the popular conception is often of young women especially being "led astray" by modern industrial employment, studies show that this is very much a myth. Most of the workers do not engage in flamboyant "modern" or "immoral" social activities, but rather are anxious to preserve their reputations.[11] However, in the Philippines and Thailand it is not uncommon for young women to have sexual relationships with boyfriends, and even to live together for long periods of time outside marriage.[12] This is not peculiar to factory workers, much less to multinational factory workers, and does not necessarily lead to the social stigmatisation of these young women. In general, the working class is less judgmental about young women's sexual behaviour than the middle and upper classes, who have a tradition of concern for women's chastity because of the importance to them of property relations and inheritance.

Some multinationals have become sensitive to local community attitudes and have changed, for instance, their personnel policies accordingly, to preserve rather than challenge traditional cultural norms, behaviour and activities of their young women workers. They have also attempted to ingratiate or align themselves with the local patriarchy, through various social programmes and mutual consultations.[13] In some countries, e.g. Morocco, foreign managers have been found to be particularly concerned to avoid offending against local social customs (Joekes, 1982, p. 33).

In general, employment in multinationals per se appears to be of only marginal importance in explaining conflicts between women factory workers and their home or host communities. The major sources of conflict arise from women leaving home and living on their own, from the over-concentration of large numbers of women migrant workers in particular host communities with inadequate public infrastructure, and from the "modern", more independent behaviour patterns common in urban areas and among women with some education and income to call their own. Patriarchal and class prejudices of local communities, rather than the behaviour of women workers or particular policies of their employers, are largely responsible for the tensions and conflicts which exist, in any event, only in very few locations. But even there controversial evidence may be obtained. Thus one survey for Malaysia noted that 85 per cent of Malay women workers in multinational electronics factories, most of them rural migrants living on their own, found their neighbours in the host community to be friendly (Zuhairah, pp. 191-2). The issue of community conflict thus appears frequently to be overestimated.

Social and cultural impact on women

In many cases, women's personal social life remains limited when they work for multinational or other factories. Yet many do manage to engage in some new social activities, permitted by their greater freedom from familial constraints and their access to both income and to new amenities available in urban areas.

Group activities are important in this connection. In Hong Kong, for example, young women workers belong to numerous formal and informal clubs and enjoy a wide variety of workplace-derived peer activities which continue until marriage (Salaff, 1981, p. 270). In Malaysia and Singapore many multinational employers provide company-sponsored social activities, with the annual dinner-dance held in luxury hotels (to which workers may, or are expected to, bring partners of the opposite sex) having the highest rate of participation. In Malaysia, one study of mostly Malay migrant workers found that only one-third participated in other company activities, although 65 per cent were satisfied with these. Sports activities - often non-existent in rural villages - were most popular. In Singapore, foreign workers have a higher rate of participation in company social activities, as the Singapore workers have easier access to the whole range of social and cultural activities that the sophisticated city offers, as well as in family social activities.

For nearly all working women, the companionship of their female workmates is an important attraction of factory work. Young school-leavers in Malaysia, for example, usually seek such jobs together, in order not only to earn income and lead an independent life for a few years, but also to maintain links with their schoolfriends after they leave school (Ackerman, 1984). In Hong Kong, peers were a primary source of enjoyable moments, providing a unique opportunity for women to learn non-familial social roles (Salaff, 1981, p. 270). In Singapore, women who had left factory employment to become full-time housewives missed the companionship of other women greatly. On the other hand, most factory women avoided domestic service because of its isolation, considered to be the worst aspect of such employment (Salaff and Wong, 1983; Wong, 1982).

Increasingly, most young women factory workers meet their future spouses through the workplace or group social activities outside the workplace (more important in the case of heavily female-intensive industries). They select their own spouses, and have the opportunity to get to know them, and in some cases even to live together, before marriage, unlike the traditional arranged marriage. Increasingly, these young men are also urban blue-collar workers, including industrail workers, who are considered more desirable marriage partners than farmers in the village, even where the latter may own some land (Ackerman, 1984). Marriage between the young male and female factory workers forms a new industrial working class and confirms the initially temporary move of rural young women away from the countryside to the city.[14]

In some ways, women's social and cultural values change as a result of factory employment and its correlates - urban residence, independent living, the earning of a wage, etc. - but in other ways they remain unchanged. A study of 2,000 women electronics factory workers in Malaysia found that the women preferred the urban way of life to family work in the peasant sector.[15] However, above all, most women remain convinced that marriage and motherhood is their desired destiny. If they do not wish to continue work, marriage is the way out of hard factory labour. If they do wish to continue work, it is usually not at the expense of, but in combination with, marriage.

In this connection a survey of women working in three multinational electronics factories in Singapore found that, while maintaining many traditional values, both single and married women held many "modern" values as well. The single women felt that they belonged to the modern world where women played different roles from the past in family and society. They postponed marriage in order to enjoy their economic and personal independence for as long as possible, but marriage remained a very important life goal (Wong, 1983, pp. 101-104).

The married woman interviewed for the above-mentioned study had all chosen their own spouses (the norm in Singapore since the late 1950s), and believed that a woman nowadays had more freedom and independence in what she did, could work outside the home, and wanted only a small number of children (Wong, 1983, pp. 126-130).

In summary, women factory workers in developing countries continue to believe strongly in marriage and the family, and in the sexual division of labour within the family, with the woman bearing the brunt of the reproductive role. They also believe that women should not marry too young, but should enjoy the social benefits of working as a single person, and that they should choose their own spouses, based on love and romance. But divorce is an acceptable and, because of women's economic independence, now a feasible alternative to unhappy marriage. In some countries, such as Singapore, they believe that marriage and wage-work can and even should be combined, that one should not have too many children, and that daughters are almost as desirable as sons and should be provided with the same opportunities.[16] There are of course considerable variations by country, depending on levels of education and urbanisation, the length of industrial experience, the state of the local labour market, and indigenous culture and religion. In all cases, however, much larger change agents are at play than simply the fact that women work in multinationals and greater changes are likely to develop over time as industrialisation advances and social life also becomes more modernised.

Notes

[1] For example, Salaff (1981) (Hong Kong); Safa (1983) (Brazil).

[2] Blake and Moonstan (no date); Salaff and Wong (1983); Wong (1982); Murayama and Munoz (1979); etc.

[3] For example, Bolles (1983), p. 148 (Jamaica); Fernandez-Kelly (1983), p. 217 (Mexico); Joekes (1982), p. 63 (Morocco).

[4] Fernandez-Kelly (1983), p. 214; Berlin (1983), p. 265; Christian Conference of Asia (1981b), p. 127; Wong (1983), p. 65.

[5] Baud (1978); Christian Conference of Asia (1981b), p. 103; Salaff, p. 268; Ackerman (1984).

[6] For example, Zuhairah (1983), p. 199, reports that 69 per cent of the women electronics factory workers in Malaysia were able to spend on luxury goods, after rent, food, essentials and remittances back home to their families.

[7] See, for example, Mather (1982) for a particularly strong argument of this case.

[8] For example, in Tunisia (Baud (1978)).

[9] Salaff (1981); Salaff and Wong (1983); Wong (1982, 1983).

[10] Miralao (1980); Miralao (1984); Wong (1982).

[11] For example, Zuhairah (1983); Tan (1984).

[12] Blake and Moonstan (1980); Zosa-Feranil (1984).

[13] See, for example, Lim (1978b).

[14] For example, in Malaysia (Ong (1983)).

[15] University of Malaya HAWA project, reported in Tan (1984).

[16] See also Zosa-Feranil (1984) on the Philippines.

CHAPTER VII

SUMMARY AND CONCLUSIONS

Multinational enterprises employ slightly more than 1 million women in developing countries, globally speaking a very small proportion - i.e. much less than 1 per cent - of the total female labour force in these countries, and about 3 per cent of total world-wide multinational employment. However, this employment varies greatly from country to country and can reach significant proportions, especially in the newly-industrialising countries and in certain economic sectors in which investments by multinationals are important. Female employment in multinationals is concentrated in the manufacturing sector, followed by services with only a very small number in agriculture. The vast majority of these women workers are in low-level production and related jobs. By region, Latin America has the largest share of women employees in multinationals, followed by Asia. The typical sector and industrial sex ratio of employment is also the main determinant of the share of women in multinationals.

The share of multinationals in agricultural employment is small and declining. Women are employed, frequently with the whole family, in multinational plantations which often date from colonial times and grow such crops as tea and rubber. Their position in the plantation labour force is inferior to that of men. More recently, newer multinational agribusiness corporations growing fruit and vegetables for export have been established in some developing countries. Women are employed there as wage-labourers in picking, packing and canning operations (which are industrial sector activities and are usually dominated by women).

In the industrial sector, women are employed by multinationals in labour-intensive, mostly export-oriented manufacturing industries such as textiles, garments and electronics which are characterised by a high ratio of women. Women are mainly concentrated in the much sex-segregated production labour force, in low-skill jobs on the assembly line. In the service sector, a small elite group of women are employed in white-collar work in multinational banks and commercial establishments. Most of the women in this sector, however, are employed in low-level jobs as maids, cleaners, waitresses and salesgirls in hotels, offices and retail establishments.

In the manufacturing sector, in parts of the services sector, e.g. sales and waitressing, and in agricultural processing, the large majority of women employed by multinationals are young and single, although there is a small but significant (and apparently increasing) proportion of married women, many of whom are single heads-of-households. In agricultural plantations, in the garments industry, and in cleaning jobs, a higher proportion of older, married women with children are employed. Factory workers tend to have a higher level of education than agricultural or the average service sector workers, especially in the multinational electronics enterprises. Because of their youth, most workers have not had previous work experience, except in the garments industry where previously learned skills are more important. Many workers in the services and industrial sectors are of rural migrant origin. However, in female-dominated manufacturing for export most are not recent migrants but urban residents. The majority find their jobs in multinationals through personal kinship and friendship networks.

Terms and conditions of employment in multinationals vary widely by country, industry and company but correspond on the whole favourably with the average local enterprises. As in other enterprises they tend to be better in situations of labour shortage than of labour surplus and better in large prosperous companies from industrialised countries. Wages for women are much determined by the prevailing local market wage rates, which are usually low in absolute terms and insufficient to support the typical working-class family. But in most cases wages paid by multinationals are adequate for the worker's own support and constitute an important contribution to the rest of her family. Many benefits and leave provisions for the common woman worker are determined by local government legislation, which is, however, rarely exceeded by multinational employers. On the other hand. non-statutory benefits would appear to be usually higher in multinationals than elsewhere. Examples of long and irregular working hours, especially shift-work and night-work, are reported as features in export-oriented enterprises including multinationals in particular in export processing zones. However, where these exist they are not specific to multinationals but particular to the sector or sometimes common in the countries. While in their subjective assessment working conditions may be judged by some workers to be unsatisfactory in some multinational enterprises, they are usually felt to be satisfactory and superior to the general local standards.

In practically all cases the jobs of women production workers are low-skilled, requiring little training, and there are virtually no opportunities for promotion. Employment in large modern enterprises including most multinationals is relatively secure and protected by law, but the duration of women's employment is brief. While for some workers this may be connected with labour conditions and management policies, for the bulk it is related to sociological factors. Indeed most women leave of their own accord after a few years to devote their full-time efforts to marriage and motherhood. Women who are part of a family workforce in agriculture are more likely to continue working after marriage, as are women heads-of-households in manufacturing.

Women in the normally large multinational plantations and factories are more likely to be unionised than women in the services sector, and frequently have much higher rates of unionisation than the rest of the female wage-labour force. While industrial relations in most cases are peaceful, industrial action has taken place even where there are no unions; but workers' bargaining power is severely limited in situations of high unemployment. Nevertheless, there is no doubt that terms and conditions of employment are generally better in unionised than in non-unionised establishments.

Multinationals employ such a small proportion of the total female labour force in the developing countries that they cannot be considered a major provider of jobs for women for the Third World taken as a whole. However, in a few countries and industries where they are concentrated they can be very important employers of women, most notably in the export-oriented industries in newly industrialising countries   in Asia, for example.

Applying a _comparative_ analysis, it would appear that in all sectors multinationals provide at least marginally better terms and conditions of employment than non-multinationals. This in a few cases seems to make the women employed better-off than the average men workers. Since in large, especially multinational, enterprises wages tend to be somewhat higher than average, benefits more numerous, hours shorter, working conditions better, employment more secure, unionisation easier and more likely, it is not surprising that a majority of the women workers in most places are satisfied with their jobs. Employment in multinationals is often clearly preferred to other alternatives for young women - where these exist. Incomes are high enough to permit substantial contributions to the family, which increases women's power, status and freedom within the family.

Women's work in industry in fact seems to strengthen the working-class family and gives it more opportunities for upward mobility. Women themselves enjoy a greater degree of independence and a wider range of consumption and social activities than were previously open to them in the traditional poor, conservative and patriarchal societies; and in many cases their social status is enhanced. Yet their personal behaviour and values have changed little as a consequence of their employment in modern multinational and other enterprises, with marriage and motherhood remaining the primary goals and foci of their lives. In rare cases, conflicts may develop with host communities where patriarchal authorities and others - threatened by women's wage employment outside the home - may protest against the assumed "moral dangers" of industrial employment.

Applying a _historical_ or _longitudinal_ analysis, it is clear that multinational wage employment, where available, has tended to improve women's working and living conditions and has expanded their opportunities and horizons in comparison with their past situations in most countries. Terms and conditions of employment also continue to improve over time, for individual workers and for the particular group, so long as the multinational remains (which the vast majority do), and especially as more multinationals enter the countries. The changes that wage employment in multinational and other enterprises introduces into women's lives and families also become more extensive and entrenched, the longer that such employment has been established.

Applying a <u>multivariate</u> analysis, it is clear, however, that in most cases the presence of modern multinational enterprises only makes a marginal, albeit positive, difference to existing local employment conditions. It is the provision of wage employment in whatever enterprises for women which is most important, and in most countries multinationals only add little to the volume of local wage employment, even in the industrial sector. The standard for employment conditions, including wages, is basically set by the local labour market. Where it is tight, employment conditions are better; where it is slack, employment conditions are negatively affected. In this connection, multinational enterprises largely reflect the prevailing local circumstances, and are usually too small an influence to affect them outside their own establishments. Where employment conditions in multinationals are better than in the average enterprises this is usually due to their larger size and prosperity compared to the local enterprises than it is to multinationality <u>per se</u> though there is an obvious correlation between these variables. And in some aspects, such as safety and health standards, multinationals often take their international experience into account. However, besides the local labour market, host government policies, the national socio-economic environment, and indigenous cultural traditions have on the whole a greater impact on women's employment conditions in industry and their effects on women's quality of working life than the pure fact that the employer is a multinational. These historically- and situationally-specific factors explain the wide diversity that can be found among developing host countries in the women's employment situation in multinationals.

From an <u>individual</u> perspective, multinational wage employment is a boon to most women who participate in it relative to their available alternatives. From a <u>social</u> perspective, such employment is in most countries insufficiently large and widespread to have a global impact on women or on society as a whole, compared to the much larger phenomenon of women's wage employment in general. Modern employment for women in multinational and other enterprises does not fundamentally disrupt, in most cases, but does modify traditional culture and society. Multinational employment of women, especially in the industrial sector, expands the working class and integrates more women into it. It also tends to increase the organisation of the workers for which large companies offer new opportunities and challenges. From a <u>national</u> development perspective, multinationals generate modern employment opportunities especially where they are export-oriented and may be net earners of foreign exchange even if these influences are insuffucient to change the prospects of the national labour market and the national economy in most of the developing countries.

From a <u>feminist</u> perspective, multinational employment for women, like all wage employment, especially in the modern industrial sector, weakens but does not usually destroy patriarchal structures which have traditionally subordinated women in most countries. It increases women's independence, power and status within the family and society, but does not liberate them from the primacy of the reproductive role, which is fundamentally linked to the sexual division of labour and sexual inequality in developing as well as in developed countries.

There clearly exists a need to improve the position of women workers whether employed in national or multinational enterprises in developing countries - firstly, as workers, and secondly, as women who still occupy a subordinate position in society. The analysis in this report has pointed out a great diversity in individual situations, with differences by country and location but more often overwhelming similarities in women's position both inside and outside multinationals.

From these, several types of policies seem to suggest themselves. Firstly, unionism would need to be strengthened in many cases, which among other things implies that restrictive legislation where it exists would have to be abandoned (e.g. as regards some export processing zones). The evidence suggests that a restrictive legislation does not necessarily attract foreign investments, so that apart from a human rights' dimension, this policy is also not justified from an economic point of view. Second, given the already respectable rate of unionisation among women industrial workers (including in most multinationals), greater influence and leadership by women themselves in unions would help to establish priorities felt by them (e.g. as regards wage inequalities, career prospects, measures to make working and family responsibilities more compatible, etc.). At the same time, increased participation of women in unions may help to increase women's commitment to the labour force and may encourage, for instance, more women to remain longer in the labour force, even after marriage, thus creating a pattern of more stable employment. From this, an impulse for social and cultural changes could be expected which would positively affect women's position in the family and society. Unions fully integrating women can be an essential factor also for effective labour relations in multinational and other enterprises.

Multinational enterprises are agents of economic modernisation in the developing countries. As regards women's concerns, their active pursuance of policies directed towards the elimination of any sex discrimination while also taking account of development practices and social aims and structure of the country in which they operate can increase their capacity for contributing to social modernisation. This, as the present study tends to show, has not yet been fully achieved in all circumstances. Indeed, the international experience of multinationals, including that in their industrialised home countries, would make multinationals particularly well suited to contributing to the full achievement of the goal of having qualifications, skill and experience the basis for recruitment, placement, training and advancement of their staff at all levels, including women workers; and this would also be enhanced through supporting representative employers' organisations in this connection.

As the analysis in this report has pointed out that broader national conditions usually dominate the narrower enterprise conditions in determining the situation of women workers, specific national-level policies and activities can further the women's cause. These include: equal rights for women under the law, including labour law, where it does not yet exist, e.g. legislating equal wage and benefits and outlawing sex discrimination; the withdrawal of restrictive legislation for women under the guise of protection; equal educational opportunities and encouragement for women; family policies and programmes; educational programmes in schools and the mass media, to propagate sexual equality and the equal sharing of reproductive as well as productive tasks; improved training programmes and equal promotional opportunities for women workers; public and private services and other provisions to facilitate and accommodate the reproductive responsibilities of working parents, such as child-care services; flexible working schedules and part-time work possibilities for both sexes; improvement of public social infrastructure, such as housing and transportation; and, most important and difficult of all, the expansion of employment opportunities for both men and women in national development programmes.

Such policies which obviously could be applied only progressively (and some of them could be sustained by corresponding policies in multinational and other enterprises) would lead to the satisfaction of needs felt by the women workers - more jobs or employment opportunities, more promotional opportunities, etc. While some of these policies would require more funds and/or expertise than many developing countries currently have, others might be less difficult to implement for multinational management. The real barriers would often seem to be cultural and ideological ones.

In short, policies are required which would not only increase employment and labour productivity in developing countries by providing more satisfactory possibilities for women to participate in the labour force and by drawing on their untapped skills and resources, but would also help to integrate women in national development. Women who can fully participate in the labour force will not only be able to share more of the fruits of development but also to participate more meaningfully in the development process as well.

BIBLIOGRAPHY

Abraham-van der Mark, E. 1983. "The impact of industrialisation on women: A Caribbean case", in J. Nash and M.P.
Fernandez-Kelly (eds.): Women, men and the international division of labor. Albany, New York, State
University of New York Press, pp. 374-386.

Ackerman, S.E. 1979. Industrial conflict in Malaysia: A
case study of rural Malay female workers. Unpublished
manuscript, University of Malaya.

---. 1984. "The impact of industrialisation on the social
role of rural Malay women: A case study of female factory
workers in Malacca", in N. Safiah Karim, (ed.): Women,
a Malaysian focus. Kuala Lumpur, Oxford University Press,
(forthcoming).

Aguiar, N. 1983. "Household, community, national and multinational industrial development", in J. Nash and
M.P. Fernandez-Kelly, (eds.): Women, men and the international division of labor. Albany, New York, State
University of New York Press, pp. 117-137.

Alonso, J.A. 1983. "The domestic clothing workers in the
Mexican metropolis and their relation to dependent
capitalism", in J. Nash and M.P. Fernandez-Kelly (eds.):
Women, men and the international division of labor,
Albany, New York, State University of New York Press,
pp. 161-172.

AMPO: Japan-Asia Quarterly Review. 1977. Special issue
on free trade zones and industrialisation of Asia (Tokyo,
Pacific-Asia Resources Center).

Arnold, F. and Piampiti, S. 1984. "Female migration in
Thailand", in J.T. Fawcett, S.E. Khoo and P.C. Smith
(eds.): Women in the cities of Asia, migration and
urban adaptation. Boulder, Colorado, Westview Press
for the East-West Center (Honolulu), pp. 143-164.

Balai Asian Journal 1981. Special issue on "Women in Asia".
No. 4, 1981.

Baud, I. 1978. Emplois et valeurs. Effets sociaux d'indus-
tries exportatrices en Tunisie. (Jobs and values, social
effects of export-oriented industrialisation in Tunisia.)
Occasional Paper No. 4, International Relations and
Industrial Structures Project, Development Research
Institute, Tilburg University, The Netherlands.

---. 1983. *Women's labor in the Indian textile industry.* International Relations and Industrial Structures Project, Report No. 23, Development Research Institute, Tilburg University, The Netherlands.

Bello, W., O'Connor, D. and Broad, R. 1982. "Export-oriented industrialization: The short-lived illusion", in W. Bello, D. Kinley and E. Elinson: *Development debacle: The World Bank in the Philippines.* San Francisco, Institute for Food and Development Policy, pp. 127-164.

Beneria, L. and Sen, G. 1981. "Accumulation, reproduction, and women's role in economic development: Boserup revisited", in *Signs: Journal of Women in Culture and Society*, No. 2, 1981, pp. 279-313.

Berlin, M. 1983. "The formation of an ethnic group: Colombian female workers in Venezuela", in J. Nash and M.P. Fernandez-Kelly, (eds.): *Women, men and the international division of labor.* Albany, New York, State University of New York Press, pp. 257-270.

Blake, M. 1975. *Towards a better deal for young workers.* Federation of Family Planning Associations, Malaysia.

---. 1980. *A case study on women in industry.* Asian and Pacific Centre for Women and Development, Bangkok.

---. 1984. "Constraints on the organization of women industrial workers", in G.W. Jones (ed.): *Women in the urban and industrial workforce: Southeast and East Asia.* Canberra, Development Studies Centre Monograph Series, Australian National University (forthcoming).

Blake, M. L. and Moonstan, C. 1980. *Women and transnational corporations (The electronics industry, Thailand).* Mimeographed paper prepared for the Culture Learning Institute, East-West Center (Honolulu, Hawaii).

Bolles, L. 1983. "Kitchens hit by priorities: Employed working-class Jamaican women confront the IMF", in J. Nash and M.P. Fernandez-Kelly, (eds.): *Women, men and the international division of labor.* Albany, New York, State University of New York Press, pp. 138-160.

Boserup, E. 1970. *Woman's role in economic development.* London, George Allen and Unwin.

Botchie, G. 1984. Employment and multinational enterprises in export processing zones: The case of Liberia and Ghana. Multinational Enterprises Programme Working Paper No. 30. Geneva, International Labour Office.

Bradley, M. 1983. "Blue jeans blues", in W. Chapkis and C. Enloe (eds.): Of common cloth, women in the global textile industry. Amsterdam/Washington, DC, Transnational Institute, pp. 87-90.

Bustamente, J.A. 1983. "Maquiladoras: A new face of international capitalism on Mexico's northern frontier", in J. Nash and M.P. Fernandez-Kelly, (eds.): Women, men and the international division of labor, Albany, New York, State University of New York Press, pp. 224-256.

Castro, J.S. 1982. The Bataan export processing zone. Asian Employment Programme Working Papers. Bangkok, ARTEP/ILO.

Centre Tricontinental (CETRI) (no date). Free trade zones and transnational corporations in Malaysia, the Philippines and Sri Lanka. (Louvain-la-Neuve, Belgium).

Chapkis, W. and Enloe, C. 1983. Of common cloth, women in the global textile industry. Amsterdam/Washington, DC, Transnational Institute.

Chhachhi, A. 1983. "The case of India", in W. Chapkis and C. Enloe (eds.): Of common cloth, women in the global textile industry. Amsterdam/Washington, DC, Transnational Institute, pp. 39-45.

Chai S.Y. 1982. Export processing and industrialisation: The case of Singapore. Asian Employment Programme Working Papers. Bangkok, ARTEP/ILO.

Chinchilla, N.S. 1977. "Industrialization, monopoly capitalism, and women's work in Guatemala" in Signs: Journal of Women in Culture and Society, No. 1, pp. 38-56.

Christian Conference of Asia. 1981a. In clenched fists of struggle, Report of the Workshop on the Impact of TNCs in Asia. Hong Kong, Urban-Rural Mission of the Christian Conference of Asia.

---. 1981b. Struggling to survive, women workers in Asia. Hong Kong, Urban-Rural Mission of the Christian Conference of Asia.

---. 1982. The plight of Asian workers in electronics.
Hong Kong, Urban-Rural Mission of the Christian Conference
of Asia.

---. 1984. Our rightful share. Hong Kong, Urban-Rural Mission
of the Christian Conference of Asia.

Costello, M.P. 1984. "Female domestic servants in Cagayan de
Oro, Philippines: Social and economic implications of employ-
ment in a 'premodern' occupational role", in G.W. Jones,
Women in the urban and industrial workforce: Southeast and
East Asia. Canberra, Development Studies Centre Monograph
Series, Australian National University (forthcoming).

Datta-Chaudhuri, M. 1982. The role of free trade zones in the
creation of employment and industrial growth in Malaysia.
Asian Employment Programme Working Papers. Bangkok, ARTEP/ILO.

Deyo, F.C. 1984. "Export-oriented industrialization and the
structural demobilization of Asian labor movements", in
C. Bergquist (ed.): Labor in the world political economy,
Berkeley, California, Sage Publications, (forthcoming).

Dror, D. 1984. "Aspects of labour law and labour relations in
selected export processing zones", in International Labour
Review, Nov.-Dec. (forthcoming).

Edgren, G. 1982. Spearheads of industrialisation or sweatshops
in the sun? A critical appraisal of labour conditions in
Asian export processing zones. Bangkok, ARTEP/ILO.

Eisold, E. 1984. Young women workers in export industries: The
case of the semiconductor industry in Southeast Asia, mimeographed World Employment Programme research working paper;
restricted, Geneva, ILO.

Elson, D. and Pearson, R. 1980. The latest phase of the internationalisation of capital and its implications for women in
the Third World. Discussion Paper No. 150, Institute of
Development Studies, University of Sussex.

---. 1981a. "The subordination of women and the internationalisa-
tion of factory production", in K. Young, C. Wolkowitz and
R. McCullagh, (eds.): Of marriage and the market. London,
CSE Books, pp. 144-166.

---. 1981b. "Nimble fingers make cheap workers: An analysis of
women's employment in Third World export manufacturing", in
Feminist Review, No. 7, pp. 87-107.

Engracia, L. and Herrin, A.N. 1984. "Employment structure of female migrants to the cities in the Philippines", in G.W. Jones (ed.): Women in the urban and industrial workforce: Southeast and East Asia. Canberra, Development Studies Centre Monograph Series, Australian National University (forthcoming).

Enloe, C.H. 1983. "Women textile workers in the militarization of Southeast Asia", in J. Nash and M.P. Fernandez-Kelly (eds.): Women, men and the international division of labor. Albany, New York, State University of New York Press, pp. 407-425.

El-Sanabary, N.M. 1983. Women and work in the Third World: The impact of industrialization and global economic interdependence. Berkeley, California, Center for the Study, Education and Advancement of Women, University of California.

Eviota, E.U. and Smith, F.C. 1984. "The migration of women in the Philippines", in J.T. Fawcett, S.E. Khoo and P.C. Smith (eds.): Women in the cities of Asia, migration and urban adaptation. Boulder, Colorado, Westview Press for the East-West Center, Honolulu, pp. 165-190.

Fawcett, J.T., Khoo, S.E. and Smith, P.C. (eds.) 1984. Women in the cities of Asia, migration and urban adaptation. Boulder, Colorado, Westview Press for the East-West Center, Honolulu.

Fernandez-Kelly, M.P. 1980. "The 'Maquila' women", in NACLA report on the Americas. Vol. 14, No. 5, Sept.-Oct. pp. 14-19.

---. 1983. "Mexican border industrialization, female labor force participation and migration", in J. Nash and M.P. Fernandez-Kelly (eds.): Women, men and the international division of labor. Albany, New York, State University of New York Press, pp. 205-223.

Foo, G. 1985. Work and marriage: Some demographic implications of factory work for single women in peninsular Malaysia. Doctoral dissertation, Center for Population Planning, University of Michigan (forthcoming).

Ford, C. 1983. Wages, hours and working conditions in Asian free trade zones. Mimeographed paper, International Textile, Garment and Leather Workers Federation, Brussels.

Frobel, F., Heinrichs, J. and Kreye, O. 1980. The new international division of labour, Cambridge, UK, Cambridge University Press.

Fuentes, A. and Ehrenreich, B. 1983. Women in the global factory. New York/Boston, Institute for New Communications/South End Press.

Global Electronics Information Newsletter. Pacific Studies Center, Mountain View, California.

Grech, J.C. 1978. Transfer of technology and the process of integration of Malta in the internationalization of production. Doctoral thesis in political science, University of Geneva. Malta University Press, 1978.

Green, S.S. 1983. "Silicon Valley's women workers: A theoretical analysis of sex-segregation in the electronics industry labour market", in J. Nash and M.P. Fernandez-Kelly (eds.): Women, men and the international division of labor. Albany, New York, State University of New York Press, pp. 273-331.

Grossman, R. 1979. "Women's place in the integrated circuit", in Southeast Asia Chronicle No. 66, Jan.-Feb., pp. 2-17.

Hackenberg, B., Barth, G., Kuo, M.J. and Angeles, T. 1984. "Growth of the bazaar economy in Davao City, Philippines: Its significance for women's employment", in G.W. Jones (ed.): Women in the urban and industrial workforce: Southeast and East Asia. Canberra, Development Studies Centre Monograph Series, Australian National University (forthcoming).

Hancock-Benseman, M. 1979. Electronics: The international industry: An examination of U.S. electronics offshore production involving a female workforce in Southeast Asia. Working Paper, Culture Learning Institute, East-West Center, Honolulu.

Hein, C. 1981. Employment of women in Mauritian industry: Opportunity or exploitation? ILO Population and Labour Policies Programme, working paper No. 114, WEP 2-21/WP. 114.

---. 1984. "Jobs for the girls: Export manufacturing in Mauritius", in International Labour Review, Mar.-Apr., pp. 251-265.

Heyzer, N. 1982. "From rural subsistence to an industrial peripheral work force: An examination of female Malaysian migrants and capital accumulation in Singapore", in L. Beneria (ed.): Women and development, the sexual division of labor in rural societies. New York, Praeger Special Studies for the World Employment Programme of the International Labour Office, pp. 179-202.

Heyzer-Fan, N. 1981. A preliminary study of women rubber estate workers in peninsular Malaysia. ILO Rural Employment Policy Research Programme, World Employment Programme research working paper, WEP 10/WP.9.

Hong, S. 1984. "Urban migrant women in the Republic of Korea", in J.T. Fawcett, S.E. Khoo and P.C. Smith (eds.): Women in the cities of Asia, migration and urban adaptation. Boulder, Colorado, Westview Press for the East-West Center, Honolulu, pp. 191-210.

Hopkins, M. 1983. "Employment trends in developing countries, 1960-80 and beyond", in International Labour Review (Geneva, ILO), July-Aug., pp. 461-478.

Institute for Research and Development of Textile Industries 1982. Studies on the effective integration of women in the development of textile industries in Indonesia. Bandung, Indonesia.

International Labour Office. 1976. Wages and working conditions in multinational enterprises. Geneva.

---. 1978. Women in industry in developing countries. ILO Research Note, ILO/W.6/1978.

---. 1979. Women and trade unions in Asia. Background Note for the Asian Seminar on Women Workers' Participation in Trade Union Activities, Kuala Lumpur, 19-24 Sept., ILO/W.11/1979.

---. 1980a. Women's participation in the economic activity of the world. (Statistical analysis) ILO/W.3/1980. Geneva.

---. 1980b. Women in rural development, critical issues. Geneva.

---. 1981. Employment effects of multinational enterprises in developing countries. Geneva.

---. 1982a. Rural development and women in Asia. Geneva.

---. 1982b. Rural women workers in Asia. Geneva.

---. 1984a. Technology choice and employment generation by multinational enterprises in developing countries. Geneva.

---. 1984b. Social and labour practices of multinational enterprises in the textiles, clothing and footwear industries. Geneva.

---. 1984c. Safety and health practices of multinational enterprises. Geneva.

International Textile, Garment and Leather Workers' Federation 1980. The international division of labour and international trade in textiles, clothing, shoe and leather products (including outward processing). Discussion Document in Three Parts. Brussels.

---. 1983. A report on the textile, clothing and leather industries in three English-speaking East African countries. Part 1, "Malawi". Part 2, "Kenya". Part 3, "Tanzania". Brussels.

ISIS International Bulletin 1978/79. Women and work. No. 10.

---. Women in development, a resource guide for organisation and action. Geneva/Rome, ISIS International Women's Information and Communication Service.

Jamilah, A. 1980. "Industrial development in peninsular Malaysia and rural-urban migration of women workers: Impact and implications", in Jurnal Ekonomi Malaysia 1, pp. 41-60.

---. 1981a. "The position of women workers in the manufacturing industries in Malaysia, in Akademika No. 18, pp. 64-76.

---. 1981b. The adaptation process and adaptive strategies of female rural-urban migrants: The case of Malay factory girls in Malaysia. Paper presented at the Young Workers Education Project's Workshop on Social Development of Factory Workers, Universiti Sains Malaysia, Penang, 12-14 Feb.

---. 1982. "Industrialization, female labour migration, and the changing pattern of Malay women's labour force participation - An analysis of interrelatioship and implications", in Southeast Asian Studies. Vol. 19, No. 4, pp. 412-425.

---. 1984. "Migration of women workers in peninsular Malaysia: Impact and implications", in J.T. Fawcett, S.E. Khoo and P.C. Smith (eds.): Women in the cities of Asia, migration and urban adaptation. Boulder, Colorado, Westview Press for the East-West Center, Honolulu, pp. 213-226.

Joekes, S.P. 1982. Female-led industrialisation. Women's jobs in Third World export manufacturing: The case of the Moroccan clothing industry. IDS Research Reports. Institute for Development Studies, Sussex, UK.

Jones, G.W. (ed.) 1984a. Women in the urban and industrial workforce: Southeast and East Asia. Canberra, Development Studies Centre Monograph Series, Australian National University (forthcoming).

---. 1984b. "Economic growth and changing female employment structure in the cities of Southeast and East Asia", in G.W. Jones (ed.): Women in the urban and industrial workforce: Southeast and East Asia. Canberra, Development Studies Centre Monograph Series, Australian National University (forthcoming).

Jurado, E.P. 1979. Some sources of social tension in Philippine industrialization. Third World Papers Series No. 19. Quezon City, Third World Studies Center, University of the Philippines.

Karl, M. 1983. "Women and multinationals", in ISIS: Women in development. A resource guide for organization and action. Geneva/Rome, ISIS International Women's Information and Communication Service, pp. 25-40.

Karl, M. and Choi, W.C. 1983. "Resistance, strikes and strategies", in W. Chapkis and C. Enloe (eds.): Of common cloth, women in the global textile industry. Amsterdam/Washington, DC, Transnational Institute, pp. 91-97.

Kassalow, E.M. 1978. "Aspects of labour relations in multinational companies: an overview of three Asian countries", in: International Labour Review, No. 3, pp. 273-287.

Kazutaka, K. 1979. "Shift work among very young female workers in the manufacturing industry", in P.K. Chew, K.O. Zee and D.Y. Chan (eds.): Proceedings of the regional seminars on occupational health and ergonomic applications in safety control. Singapore, Society of Occupational Medicine and National Safety First Council, pp. 37-43.

Khoo, S.E. 1984. "Urbanward migration and employment of women in Southeast and East Asian cities: Patterns and policy issues", in G.W. Jones (ed.): Women in the urban and industrial workforce: Southeast and East Asia. Canberra, Development Studies Centre Monograph Series, Australian National University (forthcoming).

Khoo, S.E. and Pirie, P. 1984. "Female rural-to-urban migration in peninsular Malaysia", in J.T. Fawcett, S.E. Khoo and P.C. Smith (eds.): Women in the cities of Asia, migration and urban adaptation, Boulder, Colorado, Westview Press for the East-West Center, Honolulu, pp. 125-142.

Koo, S.Y. 1984. "Trends in female labour force participation and occupational shifts in urban Korea", in G.W. Jones (ed.): Women in the urban and industrial workforce: Southeast and East Asia. Canberra, Development Studies Centre Monograph Series, Australian National University (forthcoming).

Kumbhat, M.C. (no date). Criteria of industrial wage discrimination in Malaysia - A study in the sociology of industrialization. Discussion Paper Series, School of Comparative Social Sciences, Universiti Sains Malaysia, Penang.

Kurian, R. 1982. Women workers in the Sri Lankan plantation sector. Women, Work and Development 5. Geneva.

Kyu, S.O. 1979. "Women in industry", in P.K. Chew, K.O. Zee and O.Y. Chan (eds.): <u>Proceedings of the regional seminars on occupational health and ergonomic applications in safety control</u>, Singapore, Society of Occupational Medicine and National Safety First Council, pp. 55-56.

Lee, E. 1981. <u>Export-led industrialisation and development</u>. Singapore, Maruzen Asia for the International Labour Office.

---. 1982. <u>Export-oriented industrialisation and employment in Southeast Asia</u>. Mimeographed paper, Bangkok.

Lee, P. 1981. "Hotel and restaurant workers in the Philippines", in <u>Southeast Asia Chronicle</u>, No. 78, Apr., pp. 33-35.

Lim, L.L. 1983. <u>The role of women in the Malaysian economy</u>. Mimeo. Paper presented at the Seminar on Women in the Eighties, Wanita MCA, 13 Nov.

---. 1984. "Towards meeting the needs of urban female factory workers in peninsular Malaysia", in G.W. Jones (ed.): <u>Women in the urban and industrial workforce: Southeast and East Asia</u>. Canberra, Development Studies Centre Monograph Series, Australian National University (forthcoming).

Lim, L.Y.C. 1978a. <u>Multinational firms and manufacturing for export in less-developed countries: The case of the electronics industry in Malaysia and Singapore</u>. Unpublished Ph.D. dissertation in economics, University of Michigan, Ann Arbor.

---. 1978b. <u>Women workers in multinational corporations: The case of the electronics industry in Malaysia and Singapore</u>. Michigan Occasional Papers No. 9. Ann Arbor, Women's Studies Program, University of Michigan.

---. 1982. <u>Women in the Singapore economy</u>. Economic Research Centre Occasional Paper Series No. 5. Singapore, National University of Singapore.

---. 1983a. <u>Labour and employment issues in export processing zones in developing countries</u>. Mimeo. Paper presented at the Asian Regional Team for Employment Promotion (ARTEP), ILO Workshop on Free Trade Zones and Industrialisation in Asia, Manila, the Philippines, Feb. 2-4.

---. 1983b. "Multinational export factories and women workers in the Third World: A review of theory and evidence", in Nagat El-Sanabary, comp.: "Women and work in the Third World: The impact of industrialization and global economic interdependence. Berkeley, California, Center for the Study, Education and Advancement of Women, University of California, pp. 75-90.

---. 1983c. "Capitalism, imperialism and patriarchy: The dilemma of Third World women workers in multinational factories", in J. Nash and M.P. Fernandez-Kelly (eds.): Women, men and the international division of labor. Albany, New York, State University of New York Press, pp. 70-93.

---. 1984a. Women factory workers in Southeast Asia: Some myths. Mimeo. Paper presented at the Center for Southeast Asian Studies, University of Wisconsin-Madison.

---. 1984b. Industrial restructuring and international business in Southeast Asia. Mimeo. Paper presented at the School of Business, University of Michigan.

---. 1984c. Labour requirements of high-technology in Singapore. Mimeo. Paper prepared for the National Productivity Board, Singapore.

---. 1984d. Factory production and household reproduction in Southeast Asia: The role of family, market and the State. Mimeo. Paper presented at the Conference on Women in Development, Cornell University, 7 Apr.

---. 1984e. The impact of technological change on export-oriented industry in Southeast Asia. Mimeo.

---. 1985a. "Global factory in the global city: Labor and location in the evolution of the electronics industry in Singapore and Southeast Asia", in R. Gordon (ed.): Microelectronics in transition: Industrial transformation and social change. New Jersey, Ablex (forthcoming).

---. 1985b. Southeast Asia in global industrial restructuring. (Manuscript in preparation).

Lim, L.Y.C. and Gosling, L.A.P. 1983. Changing modes of production and the sexual division of labor in Southeast Asia. Mimeo. Unpublished monograph. Center for South and Southeast Asian Studies, University of Michigan.

Lim, L. and Pang E.F. 1981. Technology choice and employment creation: A case study of three multinational enterprises in Singapore. Multinational Enterprises Programme Working Paper No. 16. Geneva, ILO.

---. 1982. "Vertical linkages and multinational enterprises in developing countries", in World Development, Vol.10, No. 7, pp. 585-595.

---. 1984. "Labour strategies for meeting the high-tech challenge: The case of Singapore", in Euro-Asia Business Review, Vol. 3, No. 2, Apr. 1984, pp. 27-31.

Lorfing, I. 1983. "Women industrial workers in Lebanon", in N. El-Sanabary, comp.: Women and work in the Third World: The impact of industrialization and global economic interdependence. Berkeley, California, Center for the Study, Education and Advancement of Women, University of California, pp. 183-192.

Maex, R. 1983. Employment and multinationals in Asian export processing zones. Multinational Enterprises Programme Working Paper No. 26, Geneva, ILO.

Mahnida, S. 1984. "Legal problems of female workers in urban areas of Indonesia", in G.W. Jones (ed.): Women in the urban and industrial workforce: Southeast and East Asia. Canberra, Development Studies Centre Monograph Series, Australian National University (forthcoming).

Mather, C.E. 1982. Industrialisation in the Tangerang Regency of West Java: Women workers and the Islamic patriarchy. Paper presented at the Conference on Women in the Urban and Industrial Workforce: Southeast and East Asia, University of the Philippines and Australian National University, Manila, 15-19 Nov.

Mba, N.W. 1983. "Women and work in Nigeria: An historical perspective", in N. El-Sanabary, comp.: Women and work in the Third World: The impact of industrialization and global economic interdependence. Berkeley, California, University of California, pp. 169-182.

Michel, A., Agbessi-dos-Santos, H. and Diarra, A.F. 1981. Femmes et multinationales. Paris, Editions Karthala.

Mies, M. 1982. The lace makers of Narsapur. London, Zed Press for the International Labour Office.

Mingmongkol, S. 1981. "Official blessings for the 'Brothel of Asia'", in Southeast Asia Chronicle, No. 78, Apr., pp. 24-25.

Miralao, V. 1980. Women and men in development. Findings from a pilot study. Quezon City, Institute of Philippine Culture, Ateneo de Manila University.

---. 1984. "Impact of female employment on household management", in G.W. Jones (ed.): Women in the urban and industrial workforce: Southeast and East Asia. Canberra, Development Studies Centre Monograph Series, Australian National University (forthcoming).

Multinational Monitor 1983. Special issue on Women and Multinationals, Vol. 4, No. 8, Aug.

Murayama, G. and Munoz, M.E. 1979. "Caracteristicas de la mano de obra femenina en la industria maquiladora de exportacion" in Cuadernon Agrarios, Sep., pp. 57-87.

NACLA 1975. "Hit and run: U.S. runaway shops on the Mexican border", in NACLA, Latin America and Empire Report. Vol.9, No. 5. July-Aug.

---. 1977a. "Capital's flight, the apparel industry moves south", in NACLA, Latin America and Empire Report. Vol.11, No. 3. Mar.

---. 1977b. "Electronics: The global industry", in NACLA Latin America and Empire Report. Vol. 11, No. 4, Apr.

Nash, J. and Fernandez-Kelly, M.P. (eds.) 1983. Women, men and the international division of labor. Albany, New York, State University of New York Press.

Neumann, A.L. 1979. "'Hospitality girls' in the Philippines", in Southeast Asia Chronicle, No. 66, Jan.-Feb., pp. 18-22.

Nihei, Y., Levin, D.A. and Ohtsu, M. 1982. "Industrialization and employment practices in Asia: A comparative study of ten spinning factories in five Asian countries", in Economic development and cultural change Vol. 31, No.1, Oct., pp. 141-171.

O'Connor, D.C. 1983. Women workers and the changing international division of labor in microelectronics. Mimeographed paper.

Ong, A. 1983. "Global industries and Malay peasants in peninsular Malaysia", in J. Nash and M.P. Fernandez-Kelly (eds.): Women, men and the international division of labor. Albany, New York, State University of New York Press, pp. 426-439.

Paglaban, E. 1978. "Philippines: Workers in the export industry", in Pacific Research, Vol. 9, Nos. 3 and 4, Mar.-June, pp. 2-31.

Pais, H. 1980. "Employment of women in India", in Indian Labour Journal, Vol. 21, No. 4, Apr., pp. 533-544.

Pang, E.F. and Lim, L. 1977. The electronics industry in Singapore: Structure, technology and linkages. Research Monograph Series No. 7, Economic Research Centre, University of Singapore.

---. 1982. "Foreign labour and economic development in Singapore", in International Migration Review, Vol. 16, No. 3, Fall, pp. 538-576.

Perpinan, Sister M.S. (no date). Women and transnational corporations: The Philippine experience. Mimeo, Manila.

Phongpaichit, P. 1981. "Bangkok masseuses: Holding up the family sky", in Southeast Asia Chronicle, No. 78, Apr., pp. 15-23.

---. 1982a. From peasant girls to Bangkok masseuses. Women, Work and Development 2, Geneva, ILO.

---. 1982b. Southeast Asia women in industry. Paper presented at the Symposium on Women, Work and Society, organised by the Indian Statistical Institute, Delhi, 22-23 Sept.

Piampiti, S. 1984. "Female migrants in Bangkok metropolis ", in J.T. Fawcett, S.E. Khoo and P.C. Smith (eds.): Women in the cities of Asia, migration and urban adaptation. Boulder, Colorado, Westview Press for the East-West Center, Honolulu.

Pineda-Ofreneo, R. 1982. "Philippine domestic outwork: Subcontracting for export-oriented industries", in Journal of Contemporary Asia, Vol. 12, No. 3, pp. 281-293.

Rahardjo, Y. and Hull, V. 1984. "Employment patterns of educated women in Indonesian cities", in G.W. Jones (ed.): Women in the urban and industrial workforce: Southeast and East Asia. Canberra, Development Studies Centre Monograph Series, Australian National University (forthcoming).

Ramanayake, D. 1982. The Katunayake investment promotion zone: A case study. Asian Employment Programme Working Paper. Bangkok, ARTEP/ILO.

Ramos, E.T. 1976. "Filipino trade unions and multinationals", in Foreign investment and labor in Asian countries. Tokyo, Japan Institute of Labor.

Ramzi, A.S. 1983. "The multinational corporations and employment opportunities for women in Malaysia", in N. El-Sanabary, comp.: Women and work in the Third World: The impact of industrialization and global economic interdepencence. Berkeley, California, Center for the Study, Education and Advancement of Women, University of California, pp. 99-100.

Rihani, M. 1983. "Women and work in Morocco", in N. El-Sanabary, comp.: Women and work in the Third World: The impact of industrialization and global economic interdependence. Berkeley, California, Center for the Study, Education and Advancement of Women, University of California, pp. 193-198.

Robbins, L. and Siegel, L. 1980. "Mattel toys around with foreign workers", in Pacific Research, Vol. 11, No. 2, pp. 3-8.

Safa, H.I. 1981. "Runaway shops and female employment: The search for cheap labor", in Signs: Journal of Women in Culture and Society, Vol. 7, No. 2, pp. 418-433.

---. 1983a. "Women and the international division of labor", in N. El-Sanabary, comp.: Women and work in the Third World: The impact of industrialization and global economic interdependence. Berkeley, California, Center for the Study, Education and Advancement of Women, University of California, pp. 3-8.

---. 1983b. "Women, production, and reproduction in industrial capitalism: A comparison of Brazilian and U.S. factory workers", in J. Nash and M.P. Fernandez-Kelly, (eds.): Women, men and the international division of labor. Albany, New York, State University of New York Press, pp. 95-116.

Salaff, J. 1981. Working daughters of Hong Kong. Filial piety or power in the family? Cambridge, United Kingdom, Cambridge University Press.

Salaff, J. and Wong, A. 1977. "Chinese women at work: Work commitment and fertility in the Asian setting", in S. Kuplinsky (ed.): The fertility of working women: A synthesis of international research. New York, Praeger, pp. 81-145.

---. 1983. "Women's work: Factory, family and social class in an industrialising order", in N. El-Sanabary, comp.: Women and work in the Third World: The impact of industrialisation and global economic interdependence. Berkeley, California, University of California, pp. 215-234.

Sassen-Koob, S. 1983. "Labor migration and the new international division of labor", in J. Nash and M.P. Fernandez-Kelly, (eds.): Women, men and the international division of labor. Albany, New York, State University of New York Press, pp. 175-204.

Sembrano, M.A. and Veneracion, C.C. 1979. The textile industry and its women workers: The Philipppine Study. Quezon City, Institute of Philippine Culture, Ateneo de Manila University.

Shoesmith, D. 1981. "The fantasy industry: Tourism and prostitution in the Philippines", in Asian Bureau Australia, pp. 4-5.

Siegel, L. 1983. "Employment of women in export assembly of high technology electronics in Asia", in N. El-Sanabary, comp.: Women and work in the Third World: The impact of industrialization and global economic interdependence. Berkeley, California, Center for the Study, Education and Advancement of Women, University of California, pp. 71-74.

Signs, Journal of Women in Culture and Society 1981. Special issue on "Development and the sexual division of labor", Vol. 7, No. 2, Winter, Chicago, University of Chicago Press.

Singhanetra-Renard, A. 1984. "Effect of female labour force participation on fertility: The case of construction workers in Chiang Mai city", in G.W. Jones, (ed.): Women in the urban and industrial workplace: Southeast and East Asia. Canberra, Development Studies Centre Monograph Series, Australian National University (forthcoming).

Siraj, M. 1984. "Islamic attitudes to female employment in industrialising economies: Some notes from Malaysia", in G.W. Jones (ed.): Women in the urban and industrial workforce: Southeast and East Asia. Canberra, Development Studies Centre Monograph Series, Australian National University (forthcoming).

Smith, W.A. 1982. The impact of Japanese foreign investment and management style on female industrial workers in Malaysia. Paper presented at the Conference on Women in the Urban and Industrial Workforce: Southeast and East Asia, University of the Philippines and Australian National University, Manila, 15-19 Nov.

---. 1983. "Japanese factory - Malaysian workers", in Jomo (ed.): The sun also sets. Kuala Lumpur, Institute for Social Analysis, pp. 250-275.

Snow, R.T. 1977. Dependent development and the new industrial worker: The case of the export processing zone in the Philippines. Unpublished Ph.D. dissertation, Department of Sociology, Harvard University.

---. 1979. "Multinational corporations in Asia: The labor-intensive factory", in Bulletin of Concerned Asian Scholars, Vol. 11, No. 1, pp. 26-29.

---. 1983a. "The new international division of labor and the U.S. work force: The case of the electronics industry", in J. Nash and M.P. Fernandez-Kelly (eds.): Women, men and the international division of labor. Albany, New York, State University of New York Press, pp. 39-69.

---. 1983b. "Export-oriented industrialization, the international division of labor, and the rise of the subcontract bourgeoisie in the Philippines", in N.G. Owen (ed.): The Philippine economy and the United States: Studies in past and present interactions. Ann Arbor, Michigan, Centre for South and Southeast Asian Studies, pp. 77-108.

Southeast Asia Chronicle 1982. No. 86. Oct.

Standing, G. 1978. Labour commitment, sexual dualism and industrialisation in Jamaica. ILO Population and Employment Working Paper No. 64. Geneva, ILO.

Staudt, K.A. 1984. "Households of women factory (Maquila) workers", in Young and Christopherson: Cuidad Juarez: Profiles of a border city. (Forthcoming.)

Subido, C.T. 1979. Employment effects of multinational enterprises in the Philippines. Research on Employment Effects of Multinational Enterprises, Working Paper No. 11. Geneva, ILO.

Tan, B.K. 1984. "Study should dispel Minah karan myths", in Business Times, Malaysia, 20 Jan.

Thong, G. 1983. Study of wage structures in HAWA-type industries. Mimeographed paper, Universiti Malaya, Kuala Lumpur.

Tongudai, P. 1984. "Women migrants in Bangkok: An analysis of their employment and earnings", in G.W. Jones (ed.): Women in the urban and industrial workforce: Southeast and East Asia. Canberra, Development Studies Centre Monograph Series, Australian National University (forthcoming).

Tse, C. 1981. The invisible control: Management control of workers in a U.S. electronics company. Hong Kong Center for the Progress of Peoples.

United Nations Industrial Development Organisation (UNIDO) (1981). Women and Industrialisation in Developing Countries.

---. 1980a. Women in the redeployment of manufacturing industry to developing countries. Working Papers on Structural Changes No. 18, UNIDO/ICIS.165.

---. 1980b. Export processing zones in developing countries. Working Papers on Structural Changes No. 19, UNIDO/ICIS.176.

---. 1983. Women in the development of textile and food processing industries. UNIDO/IS.391.

United States Agency for International Development. 1981. The social impact of agribusiness: A case study of ALCOSA in Guatemala. A.I.D. Evaluation Special Study No. 4.

Villegas, E.M. 1980. Notes on the labor code and the conditions of the industrial working class in the Philippines. The Philippines in the Third World Papers Series No. 23, Third World Studies Center, University of the Philippines.

Wagenmans, W. 1977. Hong Kong: Development and perspective of a clothing colony. Occasional Paper No. 1, International Relations and Industrial Structures Project, Development Research, Tilburg University, The Netherlands.

Weir, N. 1983. "Panel presentation on the opportunities and challenges of global economic interdependence: Implications for women", in N. El-Sanabary, Women and work in the Third World: The impact of industrialization and global economic interdependence. Berkeley, California, Center for the Study, Education and Advancement of Women, University of California, pp. 95-98.

Weiss, A.M. 1983. "Women and factory work in Punjab, Pakistan", in N. El-Sanabary: Women and Work in the Third World: The impact of industrialization and global economic interdependence. Berkeley, California, Center for the Study, Education and Advancement of Women, University of California, pp. 207-214.

Wolf, D.L. 1984. "Making the bread and bringing it home: Female factory workers and the family economy in rural Java", in G.M. Jones (ed.): Women in the urban and industrial workforce: Southeast and East Asia. Canberra, Development Studies Centre Monograph Series, Australian National University (forthcoming).

Wong, A.K. 1979. "Women's status and changing family values: Implications of maternal employment and educational attainment", in C.Y. Kuo and A.K. Wong (eds.): The contemporary family in Singapore. Singapore, University of Singapore Press, pp. 40-61.

---. 1982. Women's work and family life: The case of electronics workers in Singapore. Paper presented at the International Sociological Association 10th World Congress of Sociology, Mexico City, Aug.

---. 1983. A study of female workers in transnational electronics firms in Singapore. A Research Report submitted to the Stiftung Volkswagenwerk.

Woronoff, J. 1983. "Job creation is often the only bonus for the host", in Asian Business, June, pp. 32-38.

Yoon, S.Y. 1979. The halfway house - MNCs, industries and Asian factory girls. Draft Report, United Nations Asia and Pacific Development Institute, Bangkok.

Zosa-Feranil, I. 1984. "Female employment and the family: A case study of the Bataan export processing zone", in G.W. Jones (ed.): Women in the urban and industrial labour force: Southeast and East Asia. Canberra Development Studies Centre Monograph Series, Australian National University (forthcoming).

Zuhairah, A. 1983. Rural-urban migration: A case study of some problems confronting women factory workers in the electronics industry in Selangor. Master of Economics thesis, Faculty of Economics and Administration, Universiti Malaya, Kuala Lumpur.